RUNNING
WITH
GRACE

A Wall Street Insider's Path to True Leadership, a
Purposeful Life, and Joy in the Face of Adversity

LORI VAN DUSEN

Editing, design, and distribution by Bublish

ISBN: 978-1-647047-34-4 (eBook)
ISBN: 978-1-647047-35-1 (paperback)
ISBN: 978-1-647047-36-8 (hardcover)

To my mother, Alice Van Dusen,
for her unwavering support and love.

CONTENTS

AUTHOR'S NOTE

THUMP. THUMP. THUMP. ONE . . . FOOT IN . . . FRONT . . . of . . . the . . . other . . .

I've been running most of my adult life. Running at work. Running at home. And running with my dog, Grace, to keep it all together.

For many of us, running is a tonic. When life gets complex, confusing, or scary, a long run outside in the fresh air allows us to process, reflect, and think more clearly—all while staying in motion. But my story isn't about running; it's about moving forward when life throws you curveballs. And as one of the nation's top financial advisors, I assure you, I've been thrown my fair share.

Despite some progress, Wall Street remains a rough-and-tumble world dominated by powerful men and institutions. I fought my way to the top by thinking outside the box and working my ass off, despite the jeers, insults, and sideways glances. I hit the pinnacle of success only to have it ripped away in a legal battle with one of the biggest banks in the world. I was raped by a PhD candidate at Harvard, swindled by a business partner, and battled two life-altering medical diagnoses. None of that, though, compared with having two of the people I loved most in the world taken from me way too soon.

Of course, I'm not alone. All too many of us have survived unthinkable traumas, losses, and challenges. While the road ahead is difficult, it's the only path forward. Wisdom and strength can be found on even the most challenging journeys. I've worked hard to find that wisdom, and I think it's why I'm still standing, still moving forward, and even thriving. I'm definitely a work in progress. I stumble plenty; we all do. But I have learned that no matter what life throws our way, we can recover if we are intentional in our efforts.

Every day, no matter what the circumstances are, I do two things: I say thank you for all the blessings in my life, and I dismiss all feelings of worry or regret. If I find myself trapped in a negative thought pattern, I acknowledge the weight of it and put it aside. This allows me to find peace in even the most unsettling of circumstances. Dr. Seuss said it well:

> Life is too short to wake up in the morning with regrets. So, love the people who treat you right, forgive the ones who don't, and believe that everything happens for a reason.
>
> If you get a chance, take it.
>
> If it changes your life, let it.
>
> Nobody said it would be easy, they just said it would be worth it.

I've decided to share my journey as a businesswoman, mother, wife, philanthropist, and generally hopeful person who still has faith in humankind despite life's challenges. It has been a roller-coaster ride of hard-earned wisdom, most of which I've never talked about before publicly. But if my bumpy personal, professional, and spiritual journey can help any of you traverse life's successes and setbacks more easily, then this book will have fulfilled its purpose.

The essence of my story has been maintained, though some names have been changed and details obscured. I've built my career by staying true to myself and my values, even when Wall Street challenged them. I'm a reserved person, but I've had to stand my ground and fight for my beliefs more times than I can remember. I don't regret the extra effort. Even when I lost, I was strengthened by the battle.

No matter your profession, race, sexual orientation, education, faith, social status, or income, life will throw you curveballs. No one is exempt from this reality. Life is not fair. It was never meant to be. It's what we discover about ourselves and how we grow that define the quality and trajectory of our lives—not the experiences themselves. Adversity is an excellent teacher if you let it be. For me, discovering this truth has been quite liberating. It has allowed me to move forward and enjoy the journey, no matter what's around the next corner.

As American author, poet, and civil rights activist Maya Angelou once said, "I can be changed by what happens to me, but I refuse to be reduced by it." There is such power in her words. I hope you will find inspiration in mine.

—Lori Van Dusen

CHAPTER 1

Just Breathe

"Happiness is beneficial for the body,
but it is grief that develops the powers of the mind."

—*Marcel Proust*

BREATHE. JUST BREATHE THE AIR AROUND YOU and keep running. Nothing more, nothing less.

Moments of profound grief are always etched into our souls. I remember every detail of that particular run with my dog, Grace. It was July 2020, in the middle of the global COVID-19 pandemic. Still, a cool and perfectly lovely morning greeted us as we left the house and turned down the road. Everything along my favorite route looked exactly the same as it had before. Underneath a clear blue sky and thick canopy of green leaves, fragrant blooms of roses and rhododendrons filled my neighbors' yards, just as they always did at this time of year. The world looked beautiful and undisturbed, even though my life had been turned upside down.

Since learning about my husband's death on Father's Day, I had struggled to function. I couldn't sleep. I couldn't eat. I couldn't think. Even now, several weeks later, as I tried to run for the first time, I still couldn't fully accept the reality that Ron was gone. Even Grace knew something was terribly wrong. Her normal tail wagging as she ran by my side was replaced by worried glances. She never liked to see me cry. But still we ran. *One . . . foot . . . in . . . front . . . of . . . the . . . other . . .*

My running routine offered comfort amid the chaos. A thousand emotions and questions collided in my brain, and the ache in my chest was physical. Many years earlier, my beloved grandfather had died suddenly on Father's Day, too. Was this some cruel joke the universe was playing on me? I stopped on the side of the road, breathing hard. I bent over, put my hands on my knees, and sobbed. Grace whimpered and pulled on the leash, as if to say, *Don't stop.*

I'd overcome a lot in my life. But grieving for Ron that morning on the side of the road, I could summon nothing from my past—no strength or lessons from my life experiences. I simply collapsed and gave myself the necessary space to swim in my sorrow. I told myself that later, I would try to be grateful for the many years I'd shared with him. Later, I would try to have faith that there were divine reasons for this tragedy, even if I would never fully understand them. As Grace and I walked up the driveway to our home, my face blotchy and swollen, I clung to these simple hopes.

As anyone who has lost a loved one can attest, it's an out-of-body experience. I was a complete wreck in the months that followed. Before Ron's death, I could command a boardroom of executives and investors and speak calmly in front of an audience of thousands, but now I couldn't even make myself a simple meal. I lost a ridiculous amount of weight in a very short time.

Even though I was the mom, my sons, Conner and Cole, took care of me. They kept our family afloat. I don't know what I would have done without them. Every night Cole brought a hot cup of herbal tea into my bedroom and watched Netflix with me until I fell asleep. Meanwhile, down in the kitchen, Conner was taking care of all the paperwork and arrangements around his dad's death. Even though I was named the executor, Conner did all the work. The COVID-19 lockdown brought an unusual blessing—the boys could stay and work remotely, so I was not alone during those first terrible few months. I'm not sure I would have survived without my boys and have thought often of all the people who were isolated and alone during the pandemic.

When the first crisp mornings of September rolled in, Cole finally had to head back to his job in Los Angeles, and Conner to his home in Upstate New York. I would be on my own for the first time since Ron's death, trying to find my sea legs in an upside-down world. The three of us decided it would be best if I headed down to Florida for a few months so I wouldn't be alone in our family house with all the memories. I would only have to get through one day by myself in Rochester, and Grace would keep me company. That one day alone ended up being a blessing, a time to reflect and think about my life up to that point—where I had come from, the person I'd become, and what the next chapter of my life might be after such loss. Settling at the kitchen counter with a couple of photo albums and a big cup of tea, I began to look back . . .

CHAPTER 2

There Are No Limitations

"All limits are self-imposed."

—Icarus

NOTHING ABOUT MY CHILDHOOD INDICATED I HAD a shot in hell of becoming one of the nation's top financial advisors, managing more than $5.5 billion in assets at the peak of my career, which had been organically grown from nothing. If someone had looked into a crystal ball and said, "Lori, you will disrupt the Wall Street business model by orchestrating one of the largest exits in history from a big bank brokerage firm and ultimately form your own independent advisory business. You'll be named by *Forbes* as the No. 1 financial advisor in New York and one of America's top wealth advisors. You'll even be part of Barron's Financial Advisor Hall of Fame"—well, I would have laughed them out of the room.

I was born prematurely, a twin with a genetic blood disorder, into an average middle-class family with no special connections. Our mother divorced our biological father when my brother, Scott, and I were less than a year old, so we lived with her and our maternal grandparents for most of our childhood. As a working, single parent in the 1960s and '70s, my mom's life was not easy. From the start, she faced unprecedented challenges. When Scott and I were born seven weeks early, we were severely underweight and jaundiced and had to stay in incubators at the hospital. The doctors said I would be disabled, and Scott would probably die. Preemies rarely lived back in the '60s, but my mom took the devastating prognosis in stride. She was a survivor, and so were her babies. The family prayed. I'm happy to say that Scott and I are both thriving adults today—a living testament to the fact that miracles happen, and even doctors can sometimes be wrong.

"Mom, together, Scott and I only weighed four and a half pounds at birth," I once reminded her. "If you could fit us both in the palm of your hand, what the heck did you dress us in?"

Without missing a beat, she smiled and said, "Doll clothes." She was a resourceful lady, my mom.

Our big, boisterous, loving Italian family was led by my grandfather, Thomas Corletta, a first-generation American with only an eighth-grade education. My grandmother was very traditional and showed me how to cook. Even though we lived in a pretty rough neighborhood on Farragut Street in Rochester, New York, my brother and I were encouraged to dream big. My grandfather taught us that the only limitations in life were those we imposed on ourselves. He embodied the power of positive thinking: He dreamed, loved his family, and worked hard. His small restaurant supply business grew and profited. Ultimately, he saved enough money to build a nice house for us all in the suburbs.

Perhaps the one hint about my future career was that my grandfather *loved* the stock market. When I was seven years old, he started showing me annual corporate reports. He'd point out something in each report that had led him to invest or shy away from a particular company and its stock. Because I loved my grandfather, I tried to listen respectfully.

But back then, I believed I was destined to be an opera singer or Broadway musical star. Music was my obsession. I sang at church, performed in school musicals, and participated in community theater events. My grandfather's success also allowed me to enroll at the preparatory program at the Eastman School of Music in Rochester. I attended high school during the day and took piano and voice lessons at Eastman in the afternoons. But as happened to many girls that age, my voice matured throughout high school.

One afternoon, my music professor, a renowned soprano soloist, sat me down. "Lori, you have a beautiful voice." She paused, measuring each word as she spoke. "However, you are not . . . exceptional . . . and," she sighed, "sopranos are a dime a dozen."

I was devastated. Here was someone I looked up to and trusted completely, telling me I wouldn't make it—I wouldn't perform opera at the Met or star in a Broadway show. Many years later, I would understand that her candor was a gift. I would realize she was opening a difficult conversation that she'd had with countless other young vocalists. But that day, each word she uttered sounded like a death knell. It was clear I had a choice to make: ignore my professor, who clearly had my best interests at heart, or change course. I knew my professor was right, but it was hard to accept that my future would not be built around the arts.

When I started attending nearby Ithaca College, my classes were still in the arts, but as the years progressed, I stopped singing, practicing, performing, or even listening to classical and Broadway music. It was too painful. I changed my major to psychology.

My grandfather was there every step of the way. He was my rock and remained a joyful, kind, and loving mentor throughout this rough transition. He never let me wallow, but he also didn't try to take away my pain to make life easier. He wanted me to do the work. He had high expectations, and I certainly wasn't going to disappoint him. Of course, I'm not sure it was possible for me to disappoint my grandfather; he loved me unconditionally.

Despite his lack of formal education, my grandfather understood life at a deeper level than most doctoral candidates. He taught me to be an adventurer, to jump in headfirst and then figure out how to get back out. He pushed me to try new things and groomed me to be a leader. I was only nineteen when my dream of being a singer came to an end, but I knew I had to move on and shape a new future for myself. One piece of very valuable advice my grandfather gave me was, "Don't be a roadblock in your own life."

Okay, Grandpa, no regrets, I told myself. *Time for a life pivot.*

What would I do next? I had always been a hardworking, goal-oriented person, so it was difficult not to have a professional mission to pursue. I ended up loving psychology and learning about how and why we think and act the way we do. It was a useful and thought-provoking field of study. I immersed myself in the courses, labs, and volunteer experiences offered. I even considered becoming a clinical psychologist or psychology professor, but my heart wasn't sold on the idea. Even though I didn't pursue psychology after my undergrad years, I have used what I learned as a psychology major throughout my career. Though I wasn't sure of my career path in my younger years, I loved being in college and involving myself in dozens of extracurricular activities: student life, housing, crisis intervention, and career counseling. If there was a committee for it, I was probably on it. I was even asked to help pick the next president of the college. I became vice president of the student government and eventually won the Campus Life Award, given to students with high academic marks who enrich student life at the college.

Loving the collegiate environment, I decided to pursue university administration. *Maybe I'll be the president of a college someday,* I thought. I applied to the Harvard Graduate School of Education to get my master's, never imagining I'd get in, but I did.

CHAPTER 3

You Can Survive Even Your Darkest Hours

"Turn your wounds into wisdom."

—*Oprah Winfrey*

I'VE ALWAYS HAD A LOVE-HATE RELATIONSHIP WITH Harvard. When I arrived there in the 1980s, I was convinced I was an admissions error. Most other graduate students had put in at least a few years of work before returning to the classroom, but I dove right in after college. And since Upstate New York was all I'd ever known before moving to Cambridge, Massachusetts, I was completely out of my comfort zone. No one in my family had ever gone to college. Yet here I was at Harvard, America's oldest learning institution, which represented centuries of academic achievement.

Even the architecture intimidated me. I'm sure many other students shared my feelings. It was like walking through American history: Massachusetts Hall was built in 1720, Wadsworth House in 1726. The ornate wrought-iron gates, colonial brick buildings, golden steeples, and elegant spires constantly reminded me of the institution's gravitas and renown.

My dorm, Cronkhite Center, sat midway between Boston's Charles River and Cambridge Common, where legend has it that George Washington took command of the Continental Army in a ceremony underneath a giant elm tree (aptly named the Washington Elm). Cronkhite still houses graduate students today, and its stately three-story, colonial redbrick facade continues to impress. But when I was there, the interior was Spartan, with few of the modern conveniences the facility has today. My room barely fit a university-issued twin bed, desk, and small chair—though there was a nice-size window and a lovely courtyard outside. The women's dorm hall was on one side of the building, the men's on the other.

I didn't even realize Cronkhite was an international dorm until a young man with a strong European accent saw my name tag at a hall mixer.

"Ah, Van Dusen! You are Dutch, right?"

I explained that I was an American with Dutch ancestors, and we had a great conversation.

One of my strongest memories was the exotic smell of spices from around the world that were always wafting down the hallways. My immediate neighbors were from Columbia, Chile, Korea, and Taiwan. I was on the dorm's meal plan, but most of the hall's residents preferred cooking their own meals. I was always being invited down to one of the small communal kitchens to taste some new dish. I rarely said no to the invitation. It was fun, and I enjoyed learning about everyone's foods and traditions.

Fully embracing the adventure of my first days on campus, I marched over to Harvard Square in search of a hair salon that took walk-ins. I found a pastel-clad stylist who seated me in her chair, complimented me on my long, dark, curly hair, and suggested I'd look amazing if I cut it short.

"Sure," I said, already overwhelmed by the change of scenery. "Why not?"

Yeah, why not? I thought. *No one here knows me.*

But as long strands of my hair started falling onto the salon's tiled floor, a wave of nausea washed over me. She kept cutting—shorter and shorter.

A few days later, we had our student ID photos taken. *Shit! What have I done?* The person on my ID was not the person I'd spent twenty-one years of my life with. Her hair was—How to describe it?—spikey! I looked like a punk rock star. But who? The next time I heard "White Wedding" on the radio, I knew. I looked like a female version of Billy Idol. It would take over a year for my hair to grow back.

Ahead of my first day of graduate school, there was an extensive summer reading list to finish. Seriously, it was ridiculously long—hundreds of texts per class. No one could have read all of it in the time allotted. I certainly could not. *Which texts are the most important?* I wondered. *Which can I skim or skip?* Despite my history as a high-achieving college undergraduate sporting a 4.0 GPA, I already felt like I was barely treading water, even before stepping into the classroom. During my first class, I sat down smack in the middle of our horseshoe-style lecture room because I'd heard that students had the best chance of not being called on there. This turned out to be inaccurate.

Sure enough, the professor kicked things off by saying, "Miss Van Dusen, please open the first case for us."

You've got to be kidding, I thought, feeling my face flush. *Seriously! I'm the first person called on the first day in my very first class at Harvard. Really?* I stood up, opened the case, spoke to the best of my ability, and sat back down.

The guy seated next to me leaned over and whispered, "Great job."

I blinked, wide-eyed. "Thanks. What did I even say?"

To put it plainly, Harvard brought me to my knees. Not only was the workload immense, but the concentration of wealth, credentials, and intellectual horsepower was also formidable. To survive, I learned to wade through the vast amount of reading material and quickly disregard the useless stuff. This allowed me to get to the meat of a topic efficiently. This skill would serve me well not only at Harvard but also throughout my career. Life always produces a lot of noise. If you can get to the essence of a problem or the heart of a question quickly, you have a big advantage.

In my second semester, I fell in love with my first business courses, especially management consulting. I had two wonderful academic advisors who encouraged me and built up my confidence. I survived academically, thanks to them.

With its concentration of wealth and privilege, it seemed to me that Harvard also had a dark side, especially for women during the 1980s: sexual harassment. Decades after my graduation, I stumbled upon an online article from June 2, 2009, written by Edward-Michael Dussom and Danielle J. Kolin of *The Harvard Crimson*, entitled "Sexual Harassment Publicized, Punished, in '80s." It chronicled the class of 1984 and what appeared to be a growing number of reported incidents of sexual harassment:

> Just months after the administration drafted a new policy that outlined procedures for reporting incidents of sexual misconduct, the University publicized for the first time that it would 'reprimand' Government Professor Martin L. Kilson for allegedly attempting to kiss a freshman woman during his office hours.

> Over the next four years, the Kilson case would open a Pandora's box. Two other incidents involving faculty members and students made headlines on a campus that had, up until that point, been largely silent on the issue.

"I know that the University's policy in a way hadn't really paid attention to that issue," said University Professor Sidney Verba '53, who was the associate dean for Undergraduate Education at the time. "There was a time when that whole notion didn't even exist."

But in 1984, the University could no longer afford to ignore what seemed to be a growing problem. Students and staff began raising concerns that Harvard's sexual harassment procedures were inadequate, leaving female students, staff members and junior faculty vulnerable on a campus disproportionately male in both senior faculty and high-level administrators.

Harvard's "growing problem," as the article so lightly phrased it, pummeled me to the core of my being.

Right or wrong, I was brought up to respect teachers and professors. They were educators and role models, and as such, could do no harm. Was I naive? You bet I was. My generation trusted more than we should have. As young women in the '80s, we brought our traditional belief system into institutions and industries that had long been dominated by men. Most of them were good people, but not all.

Harvard was founded *by* men, *for* men, in 1636. From its initial days educating an all-male clergy to its rise in the eighteenth century as an institution for "the sons of the arriving mercantile elite" to grooming Boston's blue bloods during the industrial revolution, Harvard had always been devoted to the education of men. It took 284 years for the university to open its doors to women.

I identified with *The Crimson*'s article because I'd also had a Harvard professor make inappropriate advances toward me. He was a middle-aged visiting professor from a prestigious university.

Thankfully, I wasn't in any of his classes. He saw me studying in the library one day and approached me. Out of respect, I spoke with him briefly. It was something I'd soon regret; he began stalking me. I was very studious, and it was my habit to move throughout Harvard's extensive library system for a change of venue. For several months, he showed up at my three favorite library study spots. He once came over and told me that in addition to being a professor, he'd been a model. He showed me a photo of himself in a magazine where he was shirtless and dressed as a half man, half goat. That's right, he was modeling as a faun, the Greek symbol of fertility. You really can't make this stuff up. It was creepy and bizarre—but I was able to shake it off.

What happened next, however, was utterly devastating.

While *The Crimson*'s article mentions sexual harassment, the word *rape* is absent. I was raped at Harvard, and my experience was likely not isolated (though at the time, I thought it was). The world will probably never know the names of other women raped in the '80s, because most of us didn't come forward back then; I know I didn't.

I'm sharing my story now because I want women who have been sexually assaulted to know they can survive. I know all too well what it feels like to have your life hijacked by a sexual predator. For a long time, it feels like you will never be happy again. Recovery takes years and hard work, but I promise, it is possible. I am living proof.

Here is my story . . .

His name was Lucas, and when he strode into a room, at six feet two inches, his machismo was palpable. He was large and muscular, with movie-star good looks. Carly Simon's megahit "You're So Vain" from the 1970s pretty much captured the tone of this guy. He was a wealthy, privileged young man from an aristocratic family. If he hadn't been real, he could have been a fictional character in a movie. He bragged that he had two master's degrees and was working on his PhD. As a result of all his years of study, he was significantly older than I was.

Like the professor who had stalked me, Lucas first approached me while I was studying, this time at the business school library. I didn't know who he was, but it was clear right away that he was used to having the complete attention of young women. This was not the case with me. I didn't really have time for dating at Harvard; I was just trying to keep my head above water. I didn't go to parties; I just studied. I had a short, polite conversation with Lucas and told him I had to get back to my work. Like the professor, Lucas started showing up where I was studying. I had never seen him before, and now he appeared almost daily at the business school library.

Lucas was *very* persistent.

I'd done some asking around, so when he finally approached me for a date, I was ready.

"Lori," he said, dripping with charm in his Spanish accent, "we should have dinner together."

"Aren't you married, Lucas?"

He didn't even pause. "Yes, but why does that matter?"

"I think we're done, Lucas. Please leave me alone." I packed up and left the library, hopeful this would put an end to his flirtations. It did not.

I attended Harvard well before Mark Zuckerberg's version of Facebook existed. As I remember it, back in my day, the university had its own version: a printed directory—a literal book of faces that contained a photo and contact information for every student. I believe this is how Lucas found out where I lived on campus.

It was about 8:30 p.m. on a Thursday in March, and I was studying in my dorm room at my all-girls hall at Cronkhite. How Lucas got past the security desk and up to our locked hall after hours, I'll never know. So, when there was a knock that evening, I assumed it was one of my friends from the hall. I opened the door casually, saw Lucas, and tried to slam it shut. He shoved his foot in the gap, pushed the door open, and threw me down on the bed, which was only inches away. I don't remember much, but I do remember the sheer physical mass of this giant man lying on top of me. I could not move or breathe, much less speak. There was barely even time to fight. He was inside me in seconds. Gasping for breath, I managed to whisper, "If you don't get off me, I will scream at the top of my lungs." I did not know how I would actually do that with so little breath left in me, but luckily it spooked him. He pulled away and ran. His violent assault was over in a matter of minutes.

I lay frozen on my bed, numb, staring at the ceiling. My head was throbbing, as if trying to disconnect from my body. *Did that really just happen, or was it a nightmare?* I don't remember much afterward, except that the next day I told a close friend, who encouraged me to go to the campus security. I said I couldn't. I was frantic. No one would believe me. It would be my word against his. It would be humiliating. I didn't want to relive it. I wasn't strong enough. I would never finish my degree if I went after him. Harvard was hard enough. He would win, and I would lose everything I'd worked so hard to achieve. I was not going to give him that satisfaction.

The anxiety was overwhelming, but I'd made my decision. I would try to forget, keep going, and attempt to graduate. Yes, I wanted him to pay for what he had done to me, but I was pretty sure that wasn't going to happen, and trying to achieve it would probably destroy me in the process. I have always been a pragmatist. I would keep my head down and rely on my close friends for support. I was only twenty-one years old, and it was the most difficult decision I'd ever made. But making the decision not to report the rape didn't ease the trauma. My entire being was tormented and afraid. I couldn't concentrate. I tried to bury the mounting fear and emotions. I lived in a haze, running on autopilot, and retreating more and more into myself each day. I wasn't sure how long I could hold it all together.

Even without reporting Lucas's crime, my life had become unbearable. Within a few weeks, I called my mom and told her that Harvard was too hard. I did not tell her about the assault; I just said that I wanted to come home. She was confused but encouraged me to stay in school. My family was so proud of me. I felt so guilty even thinking about wanting to leave Harvard, but I had no idea how I would find the strength to make it through. No one understood that I was reliving the assault daily—every time I was alone in my room, every time I undressed for the shower, even when I saw my own distorted face in the mirror. Those distant, damaged eyes didn't seem familiar anymore. And yet I couldn't stop the internal dialogue. *Had I encouraged him? Should I have stopped talking to him earlier?* I withdrew. I struggled through the day. I was angry and paranoid about running into him on campus. I don't believe I ever told my academic advisors about the assault, but one of them, Professor Meriwether, intuitively seemed to know something was terribly wrong.

I now know that everything I was going through is common for rape victims. But back then, I just felt like I was losing my mind. Professor Meriwether and my closest friend somehow got me through my darkest days at Harvard. I stayed in school, and with their help, completed my classes. But there were plenty of moments where I almost didn't make it.

I remember one important exam where I completely froze. I couldn't remember a single answer. This had never happened to me before. Luckily, my professor could tell that something was very wrong and kindly allowed me to retake the test in his office the next morning. This was unheard of at Harvard. No one got a second chance. Fortunately, I passed the exam and his class. At the time, I didn't connect this blackout with the rape, but I now understand that it's a common problem for trauma victims. Hanging on by the thinnest of threads—and still living with debilitating feelings of shame, embarrassment, and self-loathing—I made it to graduation.

It would take many years for me to fully understand that I was blameless, and that this was the violent act of a sick man. According to the latest Center for Disease Control's National Intimate Partner and Sexual Violence Survey, nearly one in four women in the United States has experienced a completed or attempted rape during their lifetime. This is a startling statistic. I am living proof you can survive, but please don't try to do it the way I did. I chose to suffer in silence.

Some will judge me harshly for not reporting the rape at Harvard. I'm not here to defend my decision. I was just a scared kid living in a very different time. I did what I did. No one should judge any assault victim's extremely personal choice to report the crime or not. Their decisions are made while facing unspeakable realities. When it comes to seeking help, though, I beg you to do so if you have been assaulted. As a grown woman, I now understand the value of professional counseling to deal with trauma. You're gambling with your life if you try to power through it on your own. I know this firsthand because I've seen loved ones lose the gamble. Don't try to go it alone like I did. Thankfully, there are more resources available to victims today and a growing awareness of the scope and gravity of the problem.

———————
———————

My graduation day from Harvard finally arrived. I was still a complete mess but so relieved I'd made it through. On this important day, Lucas would confirm just how twisted he really was. My whole family had traveled to Boston for the ceremony. My mom, brother, and both grandparents were all there to cheer me on. After receiving my diploma, I went to find them in the crowd. We were hugging and celebrating when Lucas strode past with a smirk on his face. He came out of nowhere. Having changed all my routines to avoid him, I hadn't seen him in many months.

"Congratulations." He nodded to my family as he strode by, brimming with confidence. "She is a very *beautiful* graduate."

I'll never forget my grandmother's reaction. "Lori, who was *that*? He looks like Rudolph Valentino!" I felt physically nauseous for a moment but shook it off. I hadn't let him win. I had struggled and almost given up, but thanks to the support of my mentors and friends, I had graduated from Harvard. It would take many, many years to fully heal, but I had survived one of the darkest hours of my life.

"No one, Grandma." I shrugged with a sad smile. "He's no one."

CHAPTER 4

Curveballs Are Great Teachers

"There is no education like adversity."

—Disraeli

AFTER GRADUATION, I JUST WANTED TO GO HOME. Even though my family didn't know about the rape, I needed to rest with them in a place of safety, support, love, and joy. The door was always open at my house, and I was welcomed back with open arms. Being near my family provided a sense of normalcy, which helped me begin to heal. I slowly stepped back into my life and started to feel more like myself.

Even as a young person, I understood a few important universal truths, thanks to my grandfather. One such truth was that no one can take away who you are unless you let them. I certainly wasn't going to let Lucas ruin my life. I was still a bag of emotions—indignation, fear, sorrow, and anger—but I tried not to dwell on the horror. I felt that if I lingered in these noxious feelings, they would eat away at my very soul and ultimately immobilize me. I didn't want to live that way. I vowed to wake up each morning and put one foot in front of the other. I yearned to move forward and heal.

As I mentioned, I enjoyed the few business classes I took while enrolled in the Harvard School of Education. Though I didn't have any real work experience at the time, I was a hard worker and was asked to be team leader for a number of business case studies. This offered me a great opportunity to learn. By the time I left Harvard, I knew I wanted to try my hand at business, even though I didn't know exactly what type of business job I wanted. I was offered a position selling photocopiers at Xerox, which was founded in Rochester in 1906, and at the time of my graduation, still headquartered there. Since I wanted to live at home for a while and Xerox had one of the best training programs in the country, accepting the job was a no-brainer. Besides, back then, selling photocopiers was actually pretty cutting-edge. Oh, how times—and technology—have changed!

I didn't realize it at the time, but Xerox was way ahead of its time in promoting women and supporting diversity. When I interviewed with them, I knew it was a good fit. The company's sales approach was to put trainees into the toughest markets and see whether they could break through. In my case, that meant selling photocopiers to printing companies. That's right: I was trying to sell printing companies equipment that was likely to put them out of business. I remember lugging copiers out of the trunk of my car in all kinds of weather. They were big, bulky, and heavy. But it wasn't all bad; my upper-body strength was improving with each meeting.

Sales was actually a perfect fit for my personality, and I successfully sold photocopiers to many printing companies. Within a year, I was one of the top sales reps in the country. The job had helped me hone my interpersonal skills and become generally more confident after my humbling graduate school experience. But as I began to think about a future at Xerox, which most likely would have involved different tiers of managerial positions, I realized moving up the ladder in a huge corporation wasn't for me.

I thought I'd try finance on for size. After much research on the best Wall Street firms, I applied to Shearson Lehman Brothers' prestigious training program at the World Trade Center in New York City. The offer came a few months later, and I took it. I was told to report to my new position on July 15, 1986. But before leaving for Manhattan, life would throw me two more major curveballs.

The doctor wore a headlamp featuring small cartoon turtles. I suppose they might have distracted his younger patients, but they weren't helping this twenty-five-year-old at all. Reclining under the bright exam room lights, I gripped the armrests tightly.

"This isn't good," Dr. Mapleton said after carefully examining my neck. "You'll need imaging, but I'm quite certain it's a tumor."

A few weeks earlier, while studying some sales reports at my desk and rubbing my neck and jaw, as I always did when concentrating, I'd hit a rock-hard lump under my jawbone. *What the heck is that?* I'd wondered.

An unsettling appointment with my dentist and then an oral surgeon led to a referral to Dr. Mapleton, an otolaryngologist, a surgeon who specializes in the ears, nose, and throat. After confirmation by imaging, I was back in Dr. Mapleton's office staring at the cartoon turtles again. He diagnosed a parotid tumor growing on my trigeminal nerve near my salivary glands. Matter-of-factly, he explained that the tumor was growing right where all the nerves met that controlled my facial sensations, expressions, and chewing.

"This is very unusual in a twenty-five-year-old," Dr. Mapleton said, as if talking to himself. "It could be cancerous. We won't know until we take it out, but we must remove it. This is not going to be an easy surgery. We'll have to make an incision from your jawline all the way up and around your ear." He drew a slow, hefty line on his own neck as he spoke.

The more Dr. Mapleton talked with his robotlike delivery, the farther away I felt. His words seemed muffled, like he was speaking to me from the other end of a long tunnel. He droned on about all the risks and my bleak prognosis, including possible facial paralysis. I didn't hear a single glimmer of hope in his voice. He just kept shaking his head and talking about risks.

". . . and you're a very beautiful young woman," he continued.

What difference does that make? I wondered, staring at his cartoon turtles in disbelief. *What if I wasn't good-looking? Would that make any of this okay?*

I snapped back into the moment, got up from the exam table, shook his hand, and walked out the door with a quick wave. "Thank you very much. Got to go."

My mother was in the waiting room. "We're leaving right now. Mom, there is no way I am letting that man touch my face again."

In the days that followed, I did some research and found Dr. Robert Christie Wray Jr., professor and chair of the Division of Plastic Surgery at the University of Rochester. While I still didn't know if the tumor was cancerous, I did know I wanted a plastic surgeon to do the surgery. As Dr. Wray carefully reviewed the imaging films, I sat quietly, relieved to see no cartoon turtles anywhere in his office.

"Lori, this is not going to be cancer; you're too young. What you do have is very tricky and rare. But don't worry; we can remove the growth, and you'll fully recover. When you're older, people are going to think you had a facelift, because there's going to be a very slight scar on your jawline up around your ear."

I nodded, fully engaged. He didn't sugarcoat the challenges ahead but spoke of hope and how he would help me. *What a difference,* I thought. *Everything is going to be all right.* Dr. Wray walked me through the state-of-the-art equipment he would employ, the drainage that would happen afterward, and how we would navigate the difficult recovery together. I felt safe in his capable, compassionate hands. My surgery was scheduled for June 15, a month before I was meant to leave for my new position at Shearson Lehman Brothers.

When I came out from under anesthesia after the two-plus hours of surgery, Dr. Wray was there. "We took out the tumor. It wasn't cancer." He smiled slightly and patted my arm. "It was a tough surgery, though, Lori, and one of your nerves was damaged. I promise you'll get full functionality back. But for several months, the right side of your face is not going to have the same movement as the left. But you did great. It went very well."

I nodded groggily and fell back to sleep. I trusted Dr. Wray. He was right: the recovery was a bear, but I did get full facial movement back after a few months. Today, you'd never know I'd had surgery at all. Though I don't have complete feeling in my jawline on the right side—it sometimes feels like Novocain wearing off—I do have full control and functionality of my facial expressions and chewing.

My grandfather basically babysat me during the early days of my recuperation. At that point, I was almost unrecognizable, with all the swelling and tubes draining saliva out of my face. I slept on my mom's couch the first few days because I wasn't allowed to go up or down stairs. We no longer lived with my grandparents, so my grandfather came over and brought me water, read to me, and distracted me with stories and long conversations. He tried not to make me laugh because it hurt too much. He was my best friend, and I felt so blessed to have him in my life.

Though I was still sporting drainage tubes a few weeks after surgery, I was feeling much better and was finally allowed to drive. I headed over to my grandfather's house for Father's Day. I wanted to say thank you for everything. He was the father I'd never had—not to mention he'd basically been spoon-feeding me for the past few weeks. When I arrived, my grandmother was in the kitchen making lunch. She said Grandpa was out back cutting the lawn.

Odd, I thought. *I don't hear the mower.*

I made my way to the door, sliding it open as I called his name. "Grandpa?"

There was no response, only a few birds chirping and the distant sound of a car driving by.

I stepped outside. Next to his prized GE Elec-Trak ride-on mower, I saw him collapsed in a heap on the partially cut lawn. I screamed for my grandmother to call an ambulance. He was code blue.

The ambulance rushed him to the hospital, where my family gathered to wait for news.

"It was a pretty bad heart attack, but we're trying to stabilize him," the surgeon said to a hospital waiting room full of my family. My uncle, my mother's brother, my mom, my brother, my grandmother, and my Aunt Norma, my mother's sister-in-law were all there.

"He's dead," I told everyone after the doctor left.

"How do you know that?" my aunt snapped at me. "You don't know that! Don't say that!"

"I don't know how I know," I whispered, trying not to cry on my drainage tubes. "But he's gone." Five minutes later, the surgeon came back out and confirmed that my grandfather had passed.

———

Tom Corletta's funeral at St. Louis Church in Pittsford, New York, was a blur. I was numb. The air smelled stale, the sky was gray, and I felt like I was watching the whole event from far away. My grandfather never talked much about religion, though he was a deeply spiritual man who often read about philosophy and Christianity. He had the entire Norman Vincent Peale collection. Still, I wondered what he might have made of all the religious formalities and fuss at his funeral. A kind, humble man, he probably would have been horrified.

The huge Catholic church was overflowing with mourners all the way out into the parking lot. Finding a place to sit was nearly impossible. You'd think the church was hosting a Van Morrison concert or something; the size of the crowd was surreal.

Who are all these people? I wondered.

Through his small restaurant supply business, my grandfather knew many people in the community. When I was a kid, he took us to many restaurants, even those we couldn't afford to patronize. We saw how the wealthy lived and dined. We watched how the wait staff and chefs at these fancy restaurants conducted themselves. It provided exposure and awareness of a skillset that other lower-middle-class kids didn't often get. I didn't realize it at the time, but my grandfather was mentoring us, showing us how to think bigger than our current circumstances. His example is one of the reasons I mentor kids today.

Just about everyone my grandfather had touched in his lifetime showed up to pay tribute. Obviously, our extensive Italian family and friends attended, but also the local bank president, shopkeepers, restaurant owners, his janitor buddies, and all those he had generously lent money to but never actually collected from. To this day, when people find out that I'm Tom Corletta's granddaughter, they gush about his thoughtfulness, generosity, and great sense of humor. He was beloved, and positively impacted many lives.

Though the doctors had given me strict instructions not to cry after my surgery, I didn't care. I sobbed loudly in my church pew, half my face still frozen from the operation. Since that day, I've delivered many eulogies, but I could never have handled my grandfather's. I couldn't even speak that day. Inconsolable, the world became a less significant place without my grandfather in it. I couldn't imagine my life without him.

Not two weeks after burying my grandfather, it was time to leave for New York City. The emotional pain was so unbearable that my physical scars and facial pain from the surgery seemed inconsequential. When people ask me now how I got through that summer, all I can say is that I knew my grandfather would have wanted me to set aside my grief and focus on being and doing my best. Even in my midtwenties, his pragmatic, optimistic approach to life had shaped me. He would tell me, "Don't let emotions or circumstance paralyze you, Lori. Don't wallow. Keep putting one foot in front of the other."

I knew he was right. I couldn't go back in time and change history. My grandfather was gone. I would have to accept this sad reality and move on. But to this day, he remains the most influential person in my life. When confronted with challenges or problems, I often call upon his words of wisdom and think about how he might have handled things. He was a Depression-era kid who overcame a lot to carve out a good life for himself and his family. He taught me about the power of optimism, responsibility, and setting and achieving your goals. Whenever I think about him, I find comfort in all our great conversations and shared memories. I still want to make him proud. At the time, I channeled all my sorrow and pain into being the best person I could possibly be. I became relentless in the pursuit of my dreams.

CHAPTER 5

Do the Work Your Way

"When the winds of change blow, some people build walls and others build windmills."

—Ancient Chinese proverb

AS MY GRANDFATHER'S GRANDDAUGHTER, I LIVE by a strict set of values, including integrity and honesty. So there is no small irony in Shearson Lehman Brothers being the company that offered me my first job on Wall Street. Just about everyone in finance wanted to work for them in the 1980s. But without any formal financial training, I didn't fully understand how fortunate I was to get into their elite training program. I also, once again, did not fit the typical profile. I was a woman with an advanced degree in education whose only work experience was selling photocopiers. This made me a bit of an outsider, which would prove to be a unique advantage down the road.

When I walked in for the first day of the program in the summer of 1986, it was only a year or so before the release of Oliver Stone's acclaimed film *Wall Street*. Starring Michael Douglas, Charlie Sheen, Daryl Hannah, and Martin Sheen, the movie told the fictional story of a young stockbroker who became caught up in the unscrupulous antics of a wealthy corporate raider. The film has become an iconic portrayal of the excesses of the 1980s, and at the time, played to the world's fascination with the power, wealth, and glamour of Wall Street. The stock market was on fire, but Black Monday, which would hit in October 1987—only fifteen months after my start date—would be the biggest market correction in sixty years.

I understood little about the history or attraction of Wall Street; there was no power, wealth, or glamour in my life. I was a quiet, serious, solitary young woman with a partially frozen face. I definitely would not even have been cast as an extra in *Wall Street*. My only advantage was a need to prove myself that was so strong I was sure I could outwork anyone. Employment at Shearson Lehman Brothers was conditional on passing a slew of logic and aptitude tests as well as the commodities certification exams. As a result, my first days were in a classroom. If you failed even one exam, you were out. It was a lot like the rigorous case study work I'd done in graduate school. But I was no longer the insecure girl who felt like an admission's mistake at Harvard. I had survived violence in the darkest corners of those hallowed academic halls and had overcome plenty of other life challenges to get where I was. No one was going to take this from me. I was going to do my grandfather proud. I buried myself in test preparations that summer and fall and pushed down the grief. I would be a study robot, attempting to live exclusively in my head with hopes that my broken heart would heal. It didn't, but I passed with flying colors.

As one of Wall Street's oldest and most influential investment banks, Shearson Lehman Brothers was the love child from the merger of two of the world's most powerful financial services firms, Shearson and Lehman Brothers, neither of which exists today.

While Shearson was purchased by another investment bank in 1993, Lehman went on to become the fourth-largest investment bank and brokerage firm in the United States. But its seat near the top would not last long.

After operating for 158 years and having grown to twenty-five thousand employees, the company declared Chapter 11 bankruptcy in 2008, following the exodus of most of its clients, drastic stock losses, and credit-rating problems due partially to its involvement in the subprime mortgage crisis. With $600 billion in assets, it was the largest bankruptcy filing in US history and sent shockwaves across the country and around the world. Not only did Lehman's bankruptcy hurt its employees and clients but the organization was also said to have played a major role in the global financial crisis of 2008, the most serious one since the Great Depression of 1929. And later, when remnants of the company were merged into Smith Barney—where I would also work—some of the same people would be part of an explosive class-action sexual harassment lawsuit that became known as "the Boom Boom Room" lawsuit, filed in 1996.

Investigative journalist Susan Antilla broke the story and later wrote a book called *Tales from the Boom-Boom Room: The Landmark Legal Battles That Exposed Wall Street's Shocking Culture of Sexual Harassment.* Recapping the lawsuit on its twenty-fifth anniversary in 2021, Antilla wrote a piece for *CNN Business Perspectives* titled "Opinion: 25 years after the 'Boom Boom Room' lawsuit, Wall Street still has a long way to go." In the editorial, she recalls what many women dealt with back in the day on Wall Street:

> Their complaint described a branch office where it was acceptable for men to refer to their female colleagues as "b*tches" and "c*nts"; where the boss bellowed to the troops at an office Christmas party that the branch was "the biggest whorehouse in Garden City"; and where male brokers would assemble in a basement party room dubbed "the Boom Boom

Room" to drink, party, and engage in vulgar talk. The women also claimed that they were paid less than their male colleagues and weren't promoted as frequently.

The article said the suit was settled without admission of guilt by Smith Barney. The firm paid out $150 million, according to the women's lawyers. It was into this storied, infamous, and very male-dominated industry that I naively walked into in the mid-1980s, at a pivotal time in financial and women's history. And I didn't have a clue.

―――――
―――――

"There's your desk. Here's your phone."

That was basically all the guidance I received on my first official day of employment at Shearson Lehman Brothers. Standing in the buzzing, cubicle-laden office on the 107th floor of 2 World Trade Center, the South Tower, you could clearly see the entire Manhattan skyline through the panoramic windows. The view was surreal. New York looked like a tiny toy city. I was one of about one hundred trainees in my class—and one of only two women—who'd made it through the organization's rigorous testing. The deal was simple: if you passed the interview and all the tests, you got a job. How long that job lasted was up to you.

The room hummed with lively male voices dialing for dollars. Base pay was a draw of $24,000 a year, which meant you had to pay it back if you didn't make at least that amount in commissions. The office was up so high we could feel the building sway. During one particularly rough day in my first weeks, I was stunned to see window washers working outside, suspended well over a thousand feet above Wall Street. *Maybe my zero-salary, eat-what-you-kill job isn't so bad after all,* I thought.

But it was hard. We were sheepdogs trying to be wolves, sent out into the wild and told to hunt for deals while barely understanding what those deals looked like, much less how to find them. So, I asked myself, *What kind of people need my help? Who has financial assets but struggles to manage them?* I was used to being around older people because I had grown up living with my grandparents, so I started cold-calling the regional list of the American Association of Retired Persons (AARP). From my tiny cubicle on high, I contacted hundreds of older people of all backgrounds each week. Missing my grandfather so much, these calls were cathartic. I'm sure many of the lonelier prospects I phoned didn't mind the conversation, either. Most were willing to talk with me, and more often than not, I had genuinely great conversations. In my mind, the goal was to build trust and get a meeting, not sell a product.

"I'll be in your area on Tuesday and Wednesday," I would say as I wrapped up, and then try to set up a time to meet in person. I met individuals, couples, and families all over New York, Pennsylvania, and Connecticut. Zoom, FaceTime, and Google Hangouts didn't exist back then, so I got in my car and drove to any meeting I could get. It didn't take long for me to realize that face-to-face meetings were a powerful way to build trust. In those early years of my career, I closed most of my business in person. I kept my head down, put in the hours, drove the miles, and closed a lot of sales. A few people at the office started to notice.

One day I encountered the chairman of Shearson Lehman, the legendary Peter Cohen, as he was lighting a cigar and walking out of the elevator. As I remember it, my boss tried to introduce me to him as an up-and-coming trainee. Cohen barely acknowledged me. He looked up from his cigar with what felt like open disdain—giving off a why-are-you-bothering-me-peasant vibe—and just kept walking. I looked at my boss and shrugged, hiding my disappointment. Little did Cohen know I'd go on to be with the company for twenty years and become one of its top producers.

Even today, Wall Street is hardly a supportive environment for young women. According to a 2019 study by Deloitte, only six of the 107 largest financial firms in the world are run by women.

Even though women make up more than half the workforce of the financial services industry, only 16 percent hold senior executive positions. So, imagine what it was like back in 1987! Hostile is an understatement. Men regularly used to say things to me like, "You know, we had another woman in here once. Now she's flipping burgers." Another popular dig was, "This isn't likely to work out for you. Maybe you can become a travel agent." And my all-time favorite: "You'd be a ten if you had boobs."

Though I let none of this get to me, every day felt like I was swimming against a strong current. It was exhausting. There were no mentors or role models for females in finance back then, so I coached myself and recited daily self-affirmations. While I tried my best to stay calm and confident on the outside, inside I was struggling to stay one step ahead of constant self-doubt. I had terrible bouts of impostor syndrome. Having no formal training or education in finance didn't help. To compensate, I overprepared for meetings, rehearsed everything multiple times, triple-checked my numbers, and even role-played so I didn't appear to be the least knowledgeable person in the room. I always had this feeling that it could all be taken away from me at any moment. The credibility police would catch me and reveal my shortcomings to everyone, and poof, my job on Wall Street would be gone. It was stressful and I needed an outlet.

At the time, I was living in Battery Park City, just a few blocks from my office at the World Trade Center, so I walked to work in my suit and high heels every morning. I also loved to be outside and would run along the Hudson River in the evenings. No technology. No office. No brokers. No clients. Just me, the breeze, and the moist, salty air coming off the water. I ran in every kind of weather: rain, snow, ice—you name it. I never wanted to miss my run. It kept me sane.

As I became more successful, even the limited camaraderie of those first months faded. In the beginning, there was a level playing field because none of us had a book of business. We were all in the same precarious boat. But when I was assigned to a branch, everybody was pitted against one another. It was part of Shearson Lehman Brothers' corporate culture. They posted your sales revenue publicly so all twelve thousand brokers around the country—and everyone in your office—could see your numbers. Everyone knew exactly how much revenue you were bringing in and how many deals you were closing. But even on my best weeks, I didn't feel successful. I kept wondering what the guy above me had done to get better numbers than I had. I kept trying to improve.

In those initial few years, my in-person client appointments were always a challenge. It was easy for me to keep people on the phone; I was professional and thoroughly prepared, so I could ask meaningful questions. Conversations were authentic and flowed naturally. I never used boilerplate language or scripts. I was also a woman who was genuinely not trying to sell them anything, so I was unthreatening and refreshing. I simply asked questions and listened. People love to talk about themselves.

But when I showed up for the first in-person meeting, I could see prospective clients trying to hide their horrified expressions. I was *very* young, and they clearly expected a much older, corporate-looking person, so I intentionally tried to downplay my looks. I braided my long, dark, unruly curls and wore boring dark-colored suits. I knew I only needed fifteen minutes to win them over. The role-playing helped me nail the prospect's transition from initial shock to engagement. I remembered how my grandfather always asked open-ended questions and listened with authentic empathy. So I would ignore any resistance, take out a clean sheet of paper, start asking questions, and listen. The prospect might be judging me, but I would not judge them. I learned that if you go into a meeting—or really, any situation—with prejudgments, chances are very good that you will miss something important. My grandfather's wisdom helped me close a lot of business; I felt like he was always with me in spirit.

"What are you struggling with personally?"
"What is the biggest problem in your family?"

"What were your experiences with past investments?"

"What are you worried about if something happens to you?"

"What do you want to have happen if you're unable to work?"

"What do you really want? Perpetual wealth? A comfortable retirement? Security?"

These were the types of questions I asked prospective clients. At the same time, I asked myself, *How should this meeting end?* I developed a deliberate cadence. Perhaps this stemmed from my music training and all those practice sessions. In music, every note must be intentional. Also, each one must have articulation and expression within the context of a larger phrase. I brought this same approach into my finance career. Once I got to know the person across the table from me—having understood their problems, hopes, and dreams as well as having learned about their past investment experiences—I was in a strong position to present the right next steps and explain my value proposition. Our work together would be a partnership, I explained. I didn't realize it then, but what I was doing was unheard of at the time, and it was music to my prospects' ears. My book of business grew rapidly.

By October 1987, just before the infamous Black Monday when the Dow lost 22 percent of its value in a single day, I had been assigned to an Upstate New York branch office. The manager there was a sixty-five-year-old man named Harvey Wallace from New York City. Two days after Black Monday, Harvey got on the office loudspeaker, his gravelly voice shouting through the office, "Goddammit, fellas, get in my office *now!*"

Everyone crammed in as quickly as possible. Not missing a beat, Harvey informed us rather matter-of-factly that a broker named Saul Myers had killed himself the night before. Harvey said he'd be distributing Saul's accounts among the rest of us.

It was the most heartless thing I'd ever witnessed. No moment of silence. No respect for Saul's life or his devotion to the company. Everybody listened and then just left and went back to work. Young and still trying to heal from my grandfather's death, I stood there trying to process everything.

Harvey glared at me. "You're not getting anything, Lori, because you're a woman, you're a *goya*, and you're too young."

I snapped out of my funk and returned Harvey's stare. "Good, because I don't want anything." I turned and left the room, sick to my stomach.

Saul was an old-time broker who had been with the branch for more than thirty years. He had been kind to me in the short time I'd known him and was respected by many. It was my first year in the business, and I had no clue about the significance of Black Monday. While others were scrambling to save their life's work, I was thinking, *How often does this happen?* Unfortunately, Saul had margined a bunch of clients, and the market crash had decimated his clients' portfolios. His suicide stunned me, and Harvey's handling of the news disgusted me. I would never forget my branch manager's lack of compassion for his longtime colleague.

A number of us went to Saul's funeral and shivah, Judaism's seven-day mourning period. There, I met Saul's devastated widow, Meriam, and shared my condolences, knowing all too well that nothing could take away her pain.

When I walked out of Harvey's office that day after the announcement of Saul's death, I made it my mission to succeed without ever being handed another broker's accounts. I vowed to grow my business organically, the old-fashioned way—through hard work, discipline, and compassion. In fact, the next account I closed only a few weeks later was one of the largest pieces of business ever signed by any investment bank in the northeast up to that time. I was asked to manage the proceeds from a deal that a New York Orthodox Jewish family had made by selling their business to a large public company. The assets exceeded $30 million, which is nearly $75 million in today's dollars.

I'll never forget how my branch's management team handled the good news. I was in a crucial closing session with the family, and the meeting was running long. As a result, I missed a mandatory weekly business development meeting designed to help new advisors with sales skills and strategies. Upon my return to the office, the man who ran the meetings literally chased me around the office—scolding me in front of everyone on the floor. I assure you this would never have occurred if I'd been a man. As I remember it, everyone watched, including Harvey, but did nothing to help. Ironically, I had missed the meeting because I was actually *doing* business development—historic levels of business development, in fact.

As the branch manager, Harvey had to sign the contract paperwork for my $30 million deal only a few days after this charade. Astonished would be an understatement when it came to Harvey's reaction about the size and origins of the transaction.

"How . . . did . . . you . . . get . . . this?" is what I recall him stuttering in disbelief.

I smiled as I turned and walked out of his office. "I just listened, Harvey."

―――――

Listening and solving problems—I decided *this* was my real job—not selling financial products. From my first days in the financial industry, I knew I could make an impact if I sat on the same side of the table as my clients and helped manage their assets. Making money was never my driving force. It still isn't. For me, it has always been, "How can I best help this person?" I knew if I provided value, my relationships would strengthen, and the money would follow naturally.

At the time, my approach marked a radical shift. *No one* was managing assets; they were just selling products—mutual funds, stocks, or proprietary products, many with heavy fees. Stockbrokers were making substantial livings through commissions on these products, even though the fees and commissions often were not disclosed to clients. I did not want to work this way and felt the industry's business model was deeply flawed. Brokers could make a lot of money while their clients might not make any—in fact, their clients could *lose* money. It wasn't right. I felt a more integrated approach would be exponentially more valuable for clients and ultimately more lucrative for Shearson Lehman Brothers.

Yet in the late '80s and early '90s, this way of thinking was considered crazy; no one even knew what financial planning was. After analyzing all the client answers to my questions, I uncovered a real problem: More often than not, people were just collecting investments with no strategy. Much like today's Robinhood and Reddit investors, these brokers seemed to me just to be following the herd. They did not have anyone helping to position their assets or to align them with their objectives and goals. Identifying this problem led to a prime opportunity. The more I filled this void as a financial advisor, the more my business could grow.

My revolutionary techniques ruffled more than a few feathers along the way. In 1990, I was nearly fired for my client-first thinking. One of the top producers in my branch office, whom I remember as having a huge ego, must have felt threatened by my success. He found out that I was introducing clients to long-term care policies to cover skilled-nursing services. It was something many of my clients would need down the road as they aged, so I was simply looking out for their best interests.

I knew firsthand the importance of this type of insurance. My grandmother had needed expensive, long-term health care after my grandfather died. Because she wasn't properly covered and had not done proper estate planning, her medical bills nearly wiped out their cumulative life savings. I didn't want to see this happen to my clients. I did research on long-term care policies for them and recommended the best providers I could find. I was not paid for this work or these policies, but the jealous top producer accused me of "selling away" from the firm, even though Shearson Lehman

Brothers offered no such policies. I was able to save my job but would encounter this type of myopic thinking often throughout my career.

I was also slowly becoming aware that most of my colleagues and friends were benefiting from unbridled cronyism. I was not. I had to develop my own relationships, build my own networks, and solve my own problems. I had to work harder to achieve results, and ultimately, this made me a stronger professional. It was a real wake-up call. For the longest time, I thought everyone was working in the same slow and deliberate way that I was. In reality, most of them were taking shortcuts and scratching each other's backs with referrals, while raking in income through sales commissions on top of the undisclosed fees their clients were paying. These types of conflicts of interest were rampant, but my revenue was all "clean." The more I saw, the more I knew that the financial services industry was broken.

I started offering estate and financial planning seminars to prospective clients my very first year at Shearson Lehman. Though these are common today, back then the idea was considered bizarre. I didn't care. The seminars allowed me to have in-person meetings on a larger scale—no more driving all over the place to one-on-one meetings. Now I could talk to sizable groups. I already knew face-to-face meetings were key to building trust, but this new approach allowed me to do them at scale. I publicized free seminars with a guest attorney and would get two or three hundred people to sign up. I was good in front of people and had strong presentation skills as a result of my music training, time at Harvard, and experience selling copiers. It was an eclectic but useful résumé.

The only problems were my youth and limited expertise. The guest attorney, always an older, more experienced male, addressed this gap. As the host, I would open the seminar by introducing myself and highlighting the guest lawyer's credentials. Then I'd hand the floor over to him. After his useful and informative presentation, I would come back to the front of the room to talk about how the attorney and I worked closely together for our clients. I'd close each seminar by offering a free financial plan to anyone willing to fill out an evaluation form, which I collected at the door. Most people were willing to provide feedback, so I gathered contact information from almost everyone who had attended. Then first thing the following morning, I'd be on the phone, calling them one by one.

This was a lot of work, but it quickly amplified my business. Anyone who would take the time to attend an estate planning seminar clearly had at least some assets to protect, so the events were packed with my ideal clients. My follow-up calls usually resulted in meetings because we'd already established trust through the in-person seminar. I still have clients to this day from those early events. In fact, one of the world's most famous composers, Samuel Adler, attended one of my first seminars. He's a lovely human being, and as of this writing, ninety-three years young. He served on the faculty at Eastman and Juilliard, founded and conducted the Seventh Army Symphony Orchestra, and has published more than four hundred compositions. Everyone in compositional music knows of him, and he has been my client for decades. These are the types of enduring relationships I have. We are long-term partners.

CHAPTER 6

Love the Entire Bumpy Journey

*"A dream doesn't become reality through magic;
it takes sweat, determination and hard work."*

—Colin Powell

TRAVELING FREQUENTLY BETWEEN NEW YORK City and Rochester for work in late 1989 and early 1990, I found a haven in Rochester's Harro East Athletic Club. I worked out at the gym whenever possible to rejuvenate and find the energy to juggle my burgeoning career. A handsome, athletic man about my age often worked out nearby, but we never spoke. One cold January morning, we finished our workouts around the same time, and he strode over.

"Hi. I've been meaning to introduce myself." He politely extended his hand. "I'm Ron Boillat." We lingered at the front door of the club and talked for more than an hour. He shared that he was considering a work-related move to Texas, and I shared that I was interested in moving to New York City full-time for my job.

A few days later, Ron asked me out to dinner. Our first date was January 25, 1990—his birthday. Fittingly, he took me to the Harro East restaurant, nicknamed Harry's. With its high-end London-style pub feel, the venue was just elegant enough to impress, but just casual and warm enough to encourage conversation among two strangers. We talked for hours. I don't remember what we ate that night, but I do remember thinking, *This is the most adorable, kindest man I've ever met. Look at those dimples!* He was genuine, charming, smart, and disciplined—and I was smitten.

The next night, I cooked chicken marsala for him, and the conversation flowed again. It was if we'd known each other for years. Ron said he'd like to reciprocate and have me over to his place for dinner the next night. He put out shrimp cocktail and microwaved some Brie cheese. As someone from a big Italian family who loved good food, I suggested, "Going forward, why don't I cook and you clean the dishes?" A deal was struck, and from that point on we were inseparable. Everyone liked Ron—even my grandmother—and she never liked anyone I dated!

In March, I invited him to join me on a sailing trip in the Caribbean that I had planned before I met him. It started out as quite an adventure. Our first crew didn't have a clue what they were doing. The whole short trip was a ridiculous comedy of errors, and we didn't make it far before having to be towed back to port. A few hours later, we boarded another sailboat with an entirely new crew. This time, we made it out of the harbor successfully. The rest of the trip went swimmingly, and Ron and I had a whirlwind courtship sailing across the Caribbean. On the final day of our journey, Ron asked me to marry him.

We were married in April, just four months after our first date. Only ten people were invited to a simple ceremony, which we held at the Harro East Athletic Club Fireside Lounge. Some members of my big Italian family who didn't receive an invite were mad at me for years. Seven of my closest girlfriends found out about my marriage through a chain letter. (For those of you too young to remember, chain letters were one of the ways people spread news before mobile phones and social media.) Everyone was shocked, but Ron and I were madly in love and didn't care. We just wanted to get married right away, so we did.

———

Right from the start of our marriage, Ron and I were very active and spent a lot of time outdoors together. We played tennis. We hiked. We ran. We swam. We cycled. Even when I became pregnant the fall after our wedding, we kept exercising. When I gave birth to our son Conner, I had a very difficult labor that lasted more than forty-eight hours, including three hours of pushing. I'll spare you the gory details, but any reasonable doctor would have performed a Caesarean section, given that Conner was already three weeks late. I can't count the number of mistakes made during that delivery. I know they would never be allowed to happen today. All in all, two full days of labor demanded a type of physical endurance that I'd never experienced before. My limits—emotional and physical— were pushed beyond recognition. In the end, Conner was a forceps delivery. After it was all over, I looked at Ron and said, "You know, having survived this, I could probably run a marathon."

That is exactly how my love of marathon running began. It was ironic, because when I first started distance running, I didn't like it and felt like crap if I ran more than a few miles. But childbirth had completely altered my mindset and helped me break through some self-limiting beliefs about my physical capabilities. When I could finally walk without discomfort a month after Conner's birth, I picked up a book about a champion marathon runner who had overcome great physical hardships. His training started by walking around a track, so I started by walking around a track—every single day, even in the snow. Then I started running for five minutes and extended my run, little by little, each day. I followed all the training tips in the book and ended up running my first marathon in Toronto nine months later. After that, I kept training and running.

I believe in pushing myself to do difficult things, and marathon running is difficult. To reach the finish line, you need a plan that breaks the training and the twenty-six-plus-mile race into bite-size chunks. Even with a plan, training for a marathon requires a lot of discipline. Every week of practice, my runs got longer. My goal was to finish my first race in under four hours. The next time, it would be 3:45, and so forth. I didn't aspire to become an elite marathoner; I just wanted to challenge myself and beat my last time.

As a very fit person, Ron was always encouraging me, often referencing the movie *Rudy*, which he loved. Based on the true story of a young man who wanted to play football for the University of Notre Dame, Rudy lacked the tuition money, grades, or athletic ability required. But despite the odds, he never gave up. He had so much heart, and he finally reached his goal through hard work and determination. You regularly see this same kind of heart and commitment within the marathon culture. There's nothing else quite like it. Running marathons teaches you a lot about yourself. For me, I learned how important it is to clear my head and unplug from regular life and problems. I don't even turn on music or podcasts when I run; I just listen to my feet on the pavement. Thump. Thump. Thump. It's a beautiful way to run and very meditative—just the road and me.

Over the course of about twelve years, I finished ten marathons. Ron and I ran two of them together. Eventually, though, the injuries mounted to the point where I couldn't walk without intense pain. Much to the horror of my coworkers, I had to lie on the conference-room floor—in full business attire, no less—to attend meetings because my back was so bad. I had trouble sleeping and couldn't even get out of my car. Nevertheless, I kept running until I was told by two back surgeons that I needed spinal disk surgery. I tried every healing method out there—inversion, chiropractic, various massage techniques, acupuncture, cryotherapy—you name it—but nothing worked. I needed to stay active but was in constant pain.

I was just about to succumb to the surgery when my girlfriend, who is exceptionally athletic, told me that two spots had opened up in the hot yoga class our town was offering. "Maybe we should try it, Lori."

I was willing to try anything to avoid surgery. When we arrived at our first class, I wasn't even able to stand up straight. But by the end of the hour-and-a-half session, I could practically jog to my car. It was kind of crazy because I couldn't do many of the postures; they were too painful. It was the heat and humidity that helped. Who knew?

Hot yoga is not like most yoga classes. In an hour and a half, you strike a specific set of twenty-six positions twice in a room where the temperature is 105 degrees and the humidity is 40 percent. It's not light or fun, and there's certainly no music. Like marathon running, this style of yoga is methodical, repetitive, and requires discipline. But once you learn the positions, you don't have to think anymore; you can simply dig in and focus.

As your body learns the regimen, it becomes a deeply meditative, healing experience. Dr. David Sinclair, a geneticist and biologist widely known for his work on longevity, has written about the many antiaging benefits of putting the body through adversity. That's exactly what hot yoga does, and it worked wonders for me. I ended up attending classes every day for two years. Even when I traveled for work, I would find a hot yoga studio so I could continue my therapeutic routine. I probably could have written a hot yoga guidebook rating studios around the world. I knew the yoga positions so well that I did several classes in Japan without understanding a word the instructor was saying.

I wasn't able to run for about two years. Luckily, hot yoga filled the void and healed my back to the point where I could finally start running short distances again. I'm thankful to say that I still run today. I've often said that if I had to give up running permanently, I'd probably end up in a mental institution.

Marathon running taught me a lot about setting and meeting achievable goals. Training for and finishing a marathon transforms your outlook on many aspects of life because you accomplish things that you never thought you could do. Hot yoga taught me that when you lose or can no longer participate in one activity you love, you can always find something new to challenge you in both familiar and novel ways.

I was recently talking with my friend Eric, who is someone I had nudged to try hot yoga after he started grappling with a difficult shoulder injury. After my own amazing experience, I can't help coaxing people to join me on the mat. Eric is one of many people I have brought into the "hot room," and he has told me many times just how grateful he is for the introduction.

Eric marveled at my flexibility after a recent class. "You are so fluid, Lori!"

I laughed and told him how seven years earlier I could barely strike a single position. I recalled the way the owner of the studio looked at me that first day. I'm sure he was thinking, *This poor woman is so far gone, even hot yoga ain't gonna help her!*

Eric told me that in the brief time he'd been practicing hot yoga, his knee and shoulder pain had almost disappeared. His bloodwork had even improved. I am certainly no doctor, but I believe that the blood circulation, muscle tension and release, and microstretching of joints that hot yoga promotes is incredibly healing. There are few other ways to stimulate healing blood flow to so many essential areas of the body.

Eric never saw the physically broken person who couldn't walk a straight path seven years ago. He just saw a butterfly. Hot yoga has kept me healthy and fit, which has allowed me to manage stress much better. I don't solve problems for my clients sitting in an office in front of a computer, I do it while I'm stretching in the hot room or running out on the quiet, open road with a clear, uncluttered mind.

———————

Another reason that running, and exercise in general, became an important part of my life was to combat the side effects of beta thalassemia. If we switched bodies, you would suddenly feel like you were running on a half tank. This hereditary disease means that my red blood cells produce significantly less hemoglobin than they should. Hemoglobin is an iron-containing protein that carries oxygen throughout the body. Beta thalassemia is relatively rare and has no cure. Exercise improves my body's oxygen levels, so it is vital for my health and productivity.

In a roundabout way, I'm grateful for the diagnosis. It has forced me to care for my health without excuses. I never skipped runs while I was building my business. I never allowed myself to make the excuse, "I don't have time." Workouts were on my calendar every day. During the busiest times in my life, running allowed me to unplug and regroup. It also put me in good company. After my firm merged with Smith Barney in 1993, then-CEO Jamie Dimon and I hit the road together on more than one occasion. As I advanced up the ranks, it was nice to have his ear during our runs. I was one of eight people from a field of advisors whom he had appointed to an executive advisory board. We would talk about anything from how to make our client services more holistic to how we could attract more women to financial services.

I remember a few of our runs in particular. Once, after a board meeting in Vancouver, my husband, Ron, cycled alongside us and insisted that I wear a heart monitor, given that I was five months pregnant with our second son. Ron was afraid that Jamie and I would run too fast or for too long. His concern was well founded;

I think we ran seven miles that day. Another time in Mexico, I grabbed Jamie's shirt and kept him from falling into a huge sinkhole. For years after, we joked that I'd saved his life.

A shared devotion to running helped me build a strong rapport with Jamie. We liked each other, and I respected his values and leadership style. If I asked him for a meeting, he always made time. He didn't always agree with my ideas, but he listened. Jamie unfailingly wanted to make things better at Smith Barney. On another run, not long after I'd had my second son, Cole, I asked Jamie why the company treated maternity leave like a disability. He stopped in the middle of the road, shocked by my assessment. I explained that top producers like me were 100 percent commission based. If we weren't closing business, we weren't getting paid. But there were no accommodations for women at my level who wanted to have children.

"It's ridiculous," I said.

Once he understood, Jamie acted immediately. He challenged me to research how other major companies handled parental leave. I was happy to do so and recalled that Xerox, the company I'd sold printers for so many years earlier, was an early adopter of many of these types of programs. I shared my thoughts and findings with Jamie, and a team at Smith Barney took this idea and ran with it. Through the work of a lot of smart people there, and with Jamie's encouragement, Smith Barney created a generous and progressive parental leave policy that became a model for other financial services companies. Jamie went on to become CEO of JP Morgan Chase, the largest bank in America, and has been listed as one of the world's most influential people. I am grateful to have shared both friendship and the open road with him.

―――

The caliber of my clients continued to level up as my reach and reputation grew. One day, a client said, "Lori, nobody is doing this kind of advisory work for nonprofits or colleges. You would be good at it. I sit on a board; I'll introduce you." This is how my institutional business started. I had already proven I could foster consensus among individuals in wealthy, multigenerational families; it seemed natural that I could extend this skill to boardrooms. The main questions and challenges for large institutions, universities, and nonprofits were similar to those of the multigenerational families I'd been advising. Moving from families to institutions let me dive headfirst into the big leagues where the professional and institutional investors play.

At one point in the late 1990s, a business owner and client asked if I'd consider advising a union plan. Labor unions offer direct pensions for their members through Taft-Hartley funds, a collectively bargained pension managed by several employers and a labor union, typically from a specific industry or trade. These funds are complicated to manage because they are overseen by a committee of both employers and union reps whose money has been rolled up into a single fund. In this case, I was being asked to pitch my services to the Pipefitters and Plumbers Local 6246, a plan with tens of millions of dollars in assets. At the time, the labor union's assets were being managed by Emerson and Phelps, one of the biggest money management firms in the United States. But the fund's returns had gone through a period of underperformance, so they were interviewing new firms.

Always open to a challenge, I threw my hat in the ring. I knew it would be a very tough room, so I prepared thoroughly for my first meeting, which was with two groups of older men who were on opposite sides of the fence—union members versus employers. The union members wanted more resources, and their employers wanted to reduce benefits to keep long-term costs down. I prepared myself to manage an intimidating mix of personalities and conflicting agendas. There was no Google back then, but that didn't stop me from researching everything I could about Taft-Hartley funds and the Pipefitters and Plumbers Local 6246. Books, articles on microfiche, and law journals were all available at the library. I learned about labor laws, potential conflicts of interest, and the labor union's hot-button issues.

The primary responsibility of the fiduciary, the group overseeing the fund, is to run the plan's assets in the best interest of its participants. But the role of the fiduciary is actually more about process than outcome. You have to act with prudence and diversify the plan's assets in order to guard against large losses. You are legally obligated to compare investment vehicles and follow certain codes of conduct, especially around conflicts of interest. When I was first brought in, they weren't following these rules. It didn't seem to me that they fully understood the fiduciary laws around investing in a Taft-Hartley plan. I was able to help them address some issues.

We ended up keeping Emerson and Phelps as one of the fund's managers but moving and diversifying three-quarters of the assets. One of the founders, Todd Phelps, seemed furious that we'd moved funds. I think he was humiliated that some "nobody woman from nowhere" had forced his hand. He sent a letter saying he was going to sue me for defamation. At first, my heart stopped. *This famous, powerful investment manager is going to sue me?* But then I realized, *Wait, this must mean I'm actually relevant as a union plan advisor!* I framed the letter and still have it.

CHAPTER 7

The Outsider's Advantage

"Some of us aren't meant to belong. Some of us have to turn the world upside down and shake the hell out of it…"

—Elizabeth Lowell

"YOU'RE NOT SMART ENOUGH TO UNDERSTAND what I'm doing."

The man in front of me was eerily calm as he threw me out of his office. I was on the seventeenth floor of the famous Lipstick Building in Midtown Manhattan on an unusually warm summer day, but I had goose bumps. Not only was he trying to humiliate me, but I also knew instinctively the person in front of me could not be trusted. After trying unsuccessfully for weeks to get answers from his staff, I'd made the trip into the city and carefully planned my information-gathering session, only to be dismissed like a child.

It was the first and only time I met Bernie Madoff.

The route to that memorable meeting in 2000 began when I was referred by a client to advise a foundation with about $120 million in assets. The famed Bob Radford, chair of the group's investment committee, was leaving his advisory role to pursue other opportunities and was interviewing new advisors. A renowned mathematician, Radford had gifted a sizable amount of money to the organization's foundation.

The portfolio was extremely complicated, featuring a lot of different hedge funds. Very few people in our industry really understood hedge funds at the time, much less the varied and complicated quantitative, algorithmic, and credit strategies found in hedge fund–driven portfolios like this. When I walked in with one of my key team members to give our pitch, I knew only one person in the room, the man who had referred us. We came prepared with a complete analysis of the foundation's portfolio. Radford sat at the other end of the conference table, legs crossed, leisurely smoking a cigarette.

After a few quick icebreaker questions, he signaled that we could start our presentation.

"Let me begin by explaining what I understand about the foundation's portfolio," I said, projecting my computer screen onto the wall.

"That number is wrong," Radford interrupted.

I froze and took a deep breath. You could have heard a pin drop.

The number in question was the Sharpe ratio, a measure of risk-adjusted return. I knew it was right. He was testing us.

"No, it's correct. Here's how we calculated it." Doing the math on the spot, I maintained my cool. By this time, I was thirteen years into my career and not easily derailed. I'm also a perfectionist who walks through key details several times prior to every presentation.

"Oh yes," he nodded. "You're right. Go on . . ."

You could feel the collective sigh of relief.

We proceeded with our presentation. "Here is what's in your portfolio, and here are the implications of continuing to run the money this way. This is what we think you can do to improve."

When my colleague and I finished up, we left the room. We didn't even make it to the car before my Blackberry cell phone rang. "You're hired," Radford said, and hung up.

The real work began a couple of days later. We started digging into the institution's portfolio; it took months to fully understand. Only one thing didn't make sense: Bernie Madoff's strategy. My job was to track the group's money, but Madoff and his "staff" couldn't answer my questions, even after several phone calls and emails.

I was adamant that if the foundation kept Madoff in the portfolio, I was not covering it. Something was off. At the beginning of the month, for example, there were large-cap stock trades; at the end of the month, everything was in Treasury bills. He was producing solid returns with extremely low volatility, using a simple, conventional split-strike conversion strategy. Of all the hedge fund strategies in the foundation's portfolio, Madoff's was probably the least complicated. His portfolio should have shown volatility similar to the market, but it didn't. I kept thinking, *There is no way he can be producing these kinds of returns, doing what he claims to be doing.* At first, I believed his firm was trading on information not publicly available, but as we would all discover in the news headlines years later, it was much worse than that.

I told Radford I was not comfortable with Madoff's strategy. "I'm not going to bless this part of the portfolio, or even deal with it at all, until I meet with every single person involved." That's how I ended up visiting—and getting kicked out of—Bernie Madoff's New York office. That trip had not been fruitless, though, as Madoff's anger and lack of transparency served to reinforce my concerns, and my resolve.

"He cannot create these types of returns with this low volatility," I told one of my colleagues. "I don't know how he's doing this, but this guy is going to jail."

Unfortunately, the foundation's board wanted to have its cake and eat it, too. They said we could exit Madoff's fund if we could switch to another fund with comparable returns.

"It doesn't exist," I said.

I presented my case over and over. I pleaded. I protested. Quite honestly, I was scared. Deep down, I wanted to be wrong. I wanted someone to say, "You're an idiot, Lori. Look, we've figured out what Madoff is doing, and it's all fine! Stop worrying." But that's not what was happening. No one could make sense of it, and I felt like we were on track to drive the whole fund off a cliff. It was terrifying.

After several behind-the-scenes conversations with Radford about whether Madoff was front-running trades, I was desperate. I decided to ask this brilliant mathematician, whom I admired and respected, the million-dollar question: "Bob, do you understand what Madoff is doing?"

"No," he replied. "I really don't."

We were finally on the same page. I knew that Bob Radford's word would be much more powerful than anything I could ever say, so at the next board meeting, I asked him the same question publicly. The board finally accepted the verdict. After months of work, we were able to get the foundation's money out of Madoff's fund, saving millions of dollars in future losses.

Years later, after it had been revealed that Madoff's portfolio was a massive Ponzi scheme, the Securities and Exchange Commission investigators called me because I was on Madoff's contact list. With relief, I was able to tell them that the foundation my firm had been managing at the time was one of the few lucky ones. Let me be clear: I never knew Madoff was running a Ponzi scheme; I found out like everyone else when it became a national headline. I just knew that something was very wrong with his numbers.

For me, standing up to Bernie Madoff was a lesson in the outsider's advantage. If you follow the herd, you can lose your perspective and objectivity. It might be the easier path, but all too often, it's not the right one. If you have done the work and understand the problem, stay the course. Believe in yourself and honor your core values, even when you encounter resistance, which you will. It's part of the journey. Stay calm and focused. Push through. Persevere. You'll end up in the right place.

In order to be able to trust your gut, you must train it. Do hard things regularly. Actively spend time outside your personal and professional circles and networks. This is especially important in today's social world, where algorithms constantly feed us more of what we already like, know, and identify with. Everyone has a bias, and we all enjoy content and conversations that reinforce our beliefs, but this rarely challenges or refines our thinking. Seek out new perspectives. Learn to be comfortable being uncomfortable. It's the only way to grow.

In my business, clients hire me for my experience and professional judgment. That means it is important to tell them what they *need* to hear based on experience and careful analysis, even when it's not necessarily what they *want* to hear. It might take some courage, and there will be pushback at times, but you must tell people the truth in a tactful, diplomatic way. You must also understand who has the power in a group, and often it won't be you. This means doing the necessary work *before* a meeting to address the concerns of key people and secure their buy-in. This doesn't happen without strong relationships. When you live by your values, follow your gut, and always have your clients' best interests at heart, you build trust.

And trust is the cornerstone of all meaningful relationships.

CHAPTER 8

People Over Profits (9/11)

"In order to lead a meaningful life, you need to cherish others, pay attention to human values and try to cultivate inner peace."

—Dalai Lama

I WAS NOT IN MANHATTAN ON 9/11, BUT I WILL NEVER forget turning on CNBC with a coworker at our Rochester offices. The second plane hit the South Tower of the World Trade Center while we were watching just after nine on a particularly beautiful, bright fall morning. Speechless, we found it hard to ignore the startling juxtaposition of the dark smoke and raging red-and-orange flames coming out of the towers against the backdrop of Manhattan's cloudless, blue morning sky. It was utterly surreal—like watching a poorly set horror film. But as we all know, the events unfolding before our eyes that day were all too real.

My mind was racing. *Who is there today?*

I started calling people to see if they were okay. No one was answering. One of my closest friends, Jake, responded a few hours later by email. He said he was okay and walking to Midtown. When the towers collapsed later that morning, I was grateful to know he was out of harm's way. But I still hadn't been able to connect with many friends and colleagues. The sense of helplessness and shock was overwhelming.

I tried calling Harry, who ran a large municipal bond operation internal to Citi Smith Barney. I couldn't reach him, either. He finally called from his Jersey office twenty-four hours later and told me he was fine.

"You want to know the craziest thing, Lori? I'm sitting here overlooking Giants Stadium, but my season tickets are back in my office in the Trade Center. Guess I'll never see those again." We both laughed awkwardly, still not fully able to process the gravity of what had happened.

The days after 9/11 were filled with disbelief. I had started my career in those buildings, so very high above Manhattan, and still went to the Twin Towers for meetings regularly. As the days passed, I heard about more people I knew who were either missing, injured, or killed. Like so many others, I was glued to the news. But like only a few, I could clearly recall every inch of our offices that no longer existed. From my training and the early days of my career in the World Trade Center, I knew where people sat, where the elevator doors opened, and the view from every window . . . and I could not stop visualizing the horrors that had unfolded there. I was usually the person others turned to when they were struggling, but 9/11 reduced me to a crumbled mess.

As grounded airplanes were allowed to fly again and airports slowly reopened in the weeks after the tragedy, Ron said he was heading to Colorado to hunt up in the Rockies with some friends. I begged him not to go. I needed him and didn't want to be alone. I understood that we were having different reactions to the events of 9/11; my connection to the situation was much closer than his. Those buildings were filled with people whom I'd met or worked with—and now those buildings and way too many of those people were forever gone.

I couldn't understand why he wasn't noticing that I was on the verge of an emotional breakdown. How was I going to take care of the boys and attempt to clear my head enough to function without his support? He was leaving me in my hour of need. *Why can't he see how devastated I am?* I begged him to stay and told him they would never let him fly with a hunting bow and knives after what had just happened. But I was wrong. He took one of the first flights available when the Rochester airport reopened.

I tried my best to be empathetic and understand why Ron had felt the need to go on this trip. *Maybe he can't stand seeing me fall apart like this,* I thought. He was flying off into nature, and I was paralyzed in my house. *We are different people,* I told myself. But it was difficult for me to accept that he would pile on more pain by leaving me alone when I already felt so lost and unable to cope.

While Ron was gone, I started reading *Wild at Heart: Discovering the Secret of a Man's Soul* by John Eldredge. It's a spiritual book about relationships and helped me make at least some sense of my husband's behavior, which I found so odd and hurtful. *Ron needs to read this,* I thought. I put a copy underneath his pillow so he would find it when he came back. About ten days later, Ron arrived home and began unpacking on our bed. When he pulled out the copy of the book I'd left under his pillow, his expression was complete astonishment.

"I read it while you were gone," I said from the other side of the bed. "I think you should read it, too."

He just stood there blinking and staring at the book in his hand.

"It's a good book, Ron. I think you'll like it."

He stared at the cover a moment longer, then leaned over and pulled the exact same book out of his suitcase.

"Can you believe it, Lori?" He waved the two copies of the same book, one in each hand.

We were both stunned—talk about a signal from the universe. What were the odds? Apparently, his hunting guide in Colorado was a Christian and had recommended *Wild at Heart* to Ron. If that's not divine intervention, I don't know what is.

From that day forward, Ron worked hard on his faith. He was always a do-it-yourself guy; trying to heal himself from his broken childhood was no exception. He would do it himself. He read books, attended Bible study, learned scripture, and attended church, but never sought the professional help he so desperately needed. Was he too proud? Too confident? Too frightened? I could never get past certain walls to learn the truth. All I knew was that I loved him, and he had come home from Colorado a better man. He told me everything would be fine, and he was working on himself.

I was still in a bad place but glad to have Ron home again. It took me several weeks to be able to put in a full day's work. One of my friends said, "People need you, Lori. You can't be like this." I remember thinking, *You're right. But why do I always have to be that person?* Though my friend clearly had no idea what I was going through, I wondered why other people were allowed to fall apart but not me. It's true that I'm typically an optimist, a we-can-get-through-anything-together kind of gal, but not after 9/11. I slogged through each workday and collapsed into bed each evening.

About six weeks after the attack on the Twin Towers, just as I was starting to get my energy back, the dreaded call came from headquarters. I was asked to attend the director's advisory group meeting at the Smith Barney–Citigroup offices right across from what remained of the towers. The whole area was still a smoking pile of twisted metal and rubbish, with active body recovery underway. In my opinion, it was way too soon. But we were all told that it was time to return to work. Wall Street was determined to get back to normal, no matter what.

But nothing was normal on Wall Street—*nothing*. The whole area looked like an active war zone. The scale of the catastrophe was so unprecedented that no one had even figured out that everyone working near Ground Zero was breathing in life-threatening toxins. The terrible consequences of that would hit all too many first responders a few years later. To me, the leaders of the financial sector seemed to have only one thing on their minds: get everyone back to work. The industry was in survival mode, having been hit hard by the tragedy. The loss of people and revenue had been extreme. There was no guidebook, no historical precedent for such an event. No one knew the appropriate waiting period. Everyone just muddled through as best they could. I put on a suit for the first time, got in my car, and felt nauseous and unsettled all the way into the city.

At this point, Jamie Dimon was no longer the company's CEO. As the mergers, acquisitions, and restructurings continued, leadership at what was now Citi Smith Barney had changed. The new CEO would be at this meeting, along with several members of the bank's executive leadership team and the eight members of the advisory group, of which I had been a member for many years. I don't remember much from that luncheon meeting. I was at the table but not in the room. My most vivid memory was everyone passing around the breadbasket politely as we ate.

Human memory is fascinating. Our brains try to protect us from experiences that are too overwhelming. We compartmentalize, check out, or forget, lest we become overwhelmed by a debilitating flood of emotions. There we were in the executive dining room, passing the breadbasket, while many stories below, in clear view from the floor-to-ceiling windows only a couple of feet behind us, bodies were still being exhumed from the smoking rubble of the Twin Towers. For me, the moment was as nightmarish as the initial television footage of the attack. It brought back memories of how Saul's suicide had been announced after Black Monday as if it were nothing more than a business transaction. There was a nonchalance, a pronounced callousness toward human loss, that defined both moments. I sat at the table among my colleagues wondering, *Does my industry lack a moral conscience? How are we doing this? Does anyone else in the room feel the same way I do?* If they did, their emotions remained unspoken, as did mine. We all showed up as we were told to, functioning like robots on autopilot.

Abraham Lincoln once said, "Labor is the superior of capital, and deserves much higher consideration." I'm not sure Wall Street believes this. If it does, it certainly has an odd way of showing it. It's ironic, really. Lincoln helped create the foundation for America's banking system. I wonder what he might make of today's financial industry. Though much has changed since 9/11, my guess is that he would still recommend a reset in certain areas.

As the months passed, I had many more meetings in Lower Manhattan and stayed nearby overnight. I often ran past Ground Zero while they were still excavating. To this day, I still vividly recall the sights, sounds, and smells—the acrid air, the smoking rubble, the barbed wire everywhere, and the workers in orange safety vests and hardhats slowly sorting through the chaos.

Once I went independent and opened my own advisory firm, I stayed in Midtown and avoided Lower Manhattan. I never got used to being there after 9/11. It never felt normal again. I wouldn't return again until 2016, when my younger son, Cole, who was then in college, asked me to visit the 9/11 Memorial with him. Though I could not find the courage to go into the museum with him, I did visit the pools where all the victims are listed. It was very difficult seeing the names of so many good people that I'd known and worked with—all lost.

When we got to the top of the Freedom Tower, my son and I stood side by side, looking down on New York City on a cold, clear spring day. We were both quiet as we took in the peace and beauty of the afternoon and view. I thought about all the years I'd walked or run on the streets below, carefree and confident. Before the attack, I'd loved this part of Manhattan. It had become my second home. But after, I didn't have to be there for meetings anymore, I avoided the place as much as possible. It had taken me fifteen years to gather the courage to visit. As Cole and I stood there, all the wonderful and horrible memories washed over me. I visualized how the streets below used to look before, but the gravity of the moment weighed heavily on me. Cole was just a child on 9/11, and his reaction was very different from mine.

"Mom, don't you think it's amazing?" he turned to me and said, "You know, that you started off working in the tallest building in the world, and then later made it to the top of your industry, too?"

"I don't know." I smiled, happy he had snapped me out of my funk. "I've never really thought about myself that way. I just always worked hard and did what I thought was right. Somehow it all worked out."

I thought about my childhood dreams of being a singer and performer. I'd never even thought about working in finance. But that day, looking out from the top of the Freedom Tower, I could only think about all the people from countless walks of life and so many countries and backgrounds who had dreamed of a career on Wall Street. The Twin Towers embodied the American dream at many levels. Like Lady Liberty, the towers had been beacons broadcasting a particularly entrancing siren song. For some it was wealth, influence, and power; for others, it was just a good job that paid the bills with the promise of a brighter future. Anything seemed possible up among the clouds, high above Manhattan. Brokers, custodians, analysts, secretaries, managers, executives, window washers, and so many more—young and old, newbie and veteran, innocent and jaded, content and ambitious—they all worked alongside each other, pursuing their own American dreams. For them, September 11, 2001, was just another Tuesday, filled with opportunity and promise. The loss of so many lives, so much human potential, and so many aspirations has forever shaken me to my core.

CHAPTER 9

Get Off the Sidelines

"Courage doesn't mean you don't get afraid.
Courage means you don't let fear stop you."

—*Bethany Hamilton*

"IF I END UP DEAD IN A PARKING LOT, I HAVE SOME ideas about whom you should call," I told Ron over the dinner table one evening in 2007, my tone only half-joking.

My son Conner, who was now sixteen years old, sat across from me listening quietly as I detailed the latest round of bullying and threats. He looked worried. "Mom, why are you doing this? It's not even your job."

He was right. Unbelievably, the menace was the result of local volunteer work.

"Because," I replied calmly, "if I don't do it, who will?"

My son looked confused.

Placing my hand on his, I said, "In life, you can't just ask, 'Why me?' The better question is usually, 'Why *not* me?' Sometimes we're put in the right place at the right time with the right skills. When that happens, you can't just sit on the sidelines. You have to step up, even if it's not convenient."

And it certainly was not a convenient time for me to find myself in the middle of a nasty local political battle. I was already juggling family responsibilities while managing a complex, growing practice inside the world's largest investment bank and financial services corporation. But I *had* found myself in a fierce game of local politics—and I was *not* going to be steamrolled.

As the chairperson of the Board of Trustees of Great Lakes State College (GLSC) in western New York, I was leading the search for a new college president. Because I was interested in finding the most qualified candidate for this high-profile role, I ran afoul of the county's powerful Republican Party, which appeared to prefer having its crony installed to open the school's piggy bank and make it rain for all the party's professional colleagues and closest friends. I wasn't having it, and so they weren't having me. No matter; I wasn't about to forgo my core values just because I'd ruffled a few—maybe more than a few—high-and-mighty feathers.

Before diving into this story, a bit of background: When I first received the call from the New York governor's office in 1999, I was a complete political neophyte. Still, I was honored to be appointed to play at least a small role in the history of one of the nation's top community colleges. As a school of distinction, GLSC has consistently served its student constituents extremely well. Many of the school's stakeholders are students of color and the first in their families to pursue higher education. Everything about the appointment to the school's board of trustees seemed to align with my personal values and mission.

Interestingly, the people who eventually wanted to take me down were the same ones who initially blessed my appointment. I guess they assumed that my party registration meant I'd play ball no matter what. They had no idea I would become a Trojan horse; in the beginning, neither did I. In any case, I was appointed to the board, and after an election, happily served as vice chairperson for many years.

The first sign of trouble came when I was elected. To me, it looked like one of the top board members was using his position as a platform to run for political office. He'd even gone so far as to give stump speeches on campus. Additionally, he'd allegedly publicly let loose with an expletive-filled outburst at a GLSC sports tournament, offending a lot of people and embarrassing the school. In my opinion, he was a very difficult man, to put it politely. From where I sat, his tenure was a mess.

I asked him to meet me at a local coffee shop, knowing a public venue was the best place to deliver an important message without making a scene. After sitting down with our coffees, I recall him saying something like, "You know, Lori, you and I are a lot alike." He clearly had no clue I was about to ask him to step down. "We can do exactly what we want because we both have fuck-you money."

I practically spit out my coffee.

"No," I choked out, clearing my throat and quickly regaining my composure, "we are not!"

I told him I had received several written complaints and then proceeded to negotiate him out of his leadership position by asking him to take a leave of absence from the board while he ran for political office. He stood his ground, so I called upon the skills and confidence I'd honed during previous tough negotiations with unions and corporate and nonprofit boards. After some back-and-forth, he reluctantly agreed to step aside. But from that point on, it felt like the man had a vendetta against me. I became the board's chairperson, and within a couple of months, the long-standing president of the college announced his retirement.

"If I had to pick one person I'd want in the foxhole with me during this transition," the outgoing president told me just before his big news, "it would be you, Lori." In that moment, I wasn't quite sure what he meant. *We're not at war,* I said to myself. But soon, I fully understood his meaning. We *were* at war!

Through my financial advisory work, I'd dealt with some fairly sophisticated nonprofit organizations. But politics was clearly a very different animal. At first, the presidential search process I was overseeing followed the protocols outlined by the school's bylaws. Because the college was unionized, there were two parallel search committees consisting of different stakeholders. The committee I'd formed included city business leaders, educators, and members of the school's board of trustees. The other search committee was run by the union and faculty. Despite different agendas, both committees ended up agreeing on the same exceptional candidate after a nation-wide search. Having worked hard to get everyone to collaborate, I was very pleased. Building a consensus within large groups is one of my core strengths as a wealth manager for nonprofit and institutional endowments, and I was happy to be able to put that skill to work to support GLSC's search.

It appeared that the county politicians in office wanted to install their own local candidate, who was much less qualified, in my opinion. Their candidate didn't appear to understand anything about the school or its programs. He was a white male lawyer from the city's elite suburbs, while GLSC's student population had always been diverse and made up of at least 50 percent urban African American and Latinx students. The pure hubris of the politicians' choice riled me up. *They're not going to ruin this school for these students. I won't see their quality education watered down. No way!* Spouting off technicalities and arcane rules, the politicians sought to discredit me, our selection process, and our candidate. They even held a public forum where I was basically put on trial in an effort to get our results overturned. Though the media supported me, it felt like these politicians relentlessly targeted me for months in the local newspaper and on the evening news—and I'm talking full-blown, unveiled intimidation. It was a lot.

In the end, the local politicians won the first round. The highly skilled educator we had nominated withdrew his candidacy, saying, "This county government is going to be a problem for me." He was right. He could see the writing on the wall. The local Republican Party controlled all the purse strings, and he knew he'd be fighting an uphill battle when it came to funding important programs at the college. It was a real loss.

At first, I didn't understand what was happening. I asked myself, *Why would anybody take a local, suburban, white male lawyer and put him in charge of a nationally ranked school known for its diversity and innovation?* Looking back, I can't help but laugh at the naivete of my question. But back then it took a second to hit me. *So, this is what politics looks like close up. It's a classic power grab!*

Today, as a more seasoned professional, I understand that this is how politics works in a lot of organizations, communities, states, and countries. Leaders—no matter what their party affiliation—all too often worry more about themselves than serving their constituents. There are often layers and layers of corruption. If this concentration of power goes unchecked, things can get bad, real fast. This has happened in many places, even my hometown.

As a young professional, I watched Rochester grow closed off to diverse ideas and fresh voices. It seemed to grow more corrupt with rumors about people trading on favors, privilege, and back-scratching. It was profoundly disappointing, given the city's rich history as the birthplace of Frederick Douglass's abolitionist newspaper *The North Star* and host of the second women's rights convention in 1848. The city seemed to slowly stray from this progressive vision. I knew instinctively as a young woman in finance in the 1980s that building my career in Rochester would be nearly impossible. It was an old-money town with a powerful old boy network, especially around the institutions I was trying to reach.

I was not connected to old money, and I was not a white male. Instead, I went to New York City, where the competition was much fiercer but, in many ways, fairer. Everybody had a shot in the Big Apple. Once my career was in full swing, I traveled between New York City and my hometown and was ultimately based in Shearson Lehman's Rochester office, though none of my clients were from there. Truth is, I benefited from Rochester's rich history and educational institutions, but when it came time to make something of myself, sadly, I had to leave. Today, Rochester shows renewed interest in progressive change, and I'm hopeful that the future is bright for this special city that holds so many memories and so much history for my family and me. It's still home.

———

But back when I was part of GLSC's board, I was experiencing the rough-and-tumble of Rochester's politics up close for the first time. Once I fully understood the situation, I knew how to identify and expose the troublemakers. This is never difficult. People acting in the name of greed and hubris are easy to spot. They share a common characteristic: they all get very agitated when you question their actions. I'd seen this firsthand when I confronted Bernie Madoff in his Manhattan office back in 2000.

To stymie the powers that be, I did two things: First, I formed a sort of coalition by having countless one-on-one meetings with interested parties in the community—business leaders, faculty members, students, you name it—to explain what was going on and why it was so problematic. I met with workforce development people, CEOs, and other C-suite executives of the region's big companies, as well as local leaders who were very prominent in education. I tried to build an infrastructure of understanding. The politicians had no idea what I was up to because their arrogance and entitlement created monovision, a common ailment in politics. Second, I chose several key moments to quietly get crucial information to the media to spark investigations. I did this with a lot of care so it could not be traced back to me. This approach ensured that the truth would come out slowly and methodically.

Despite my covert operations, I was still the face of the opposition. The pressure continued. The politicians wanted me out and tried to dig up dirt on me. This was not easy because I'd always avoided conflicts of interest since they led to bad decisions. I've never been a back scratcher, and I was happy to make their job more difficult.

———

As we were walking into the climactic executive session to battle things out, the Republican Party's henchman appeared to have a warning for me. As I remember it, he leaned in close and hissed, "Pal, you don't know what you're up against."

"Just the opposite, *pal*," I retorted. "You don't know what *you're* up against."

Today, when I recall my response, it makes me laugh. But when I was in the thick of it, my reaction felt right and allowed me to release some of the built-up adrenaline coursing through my veins. What the henchman didn't realize was that I was about to surprise them with my resignation, which would trigger a series of carefully planned events that would let the dominoes start falling.

Ahead of the meeting, I had chosen to invoke what's called the Sunshine Rule in New York State. This meant it was perfectly lawful to invite all the community leaders, faculty, students, and staff to the meeting. I had planned everything very carefully. By now, my personal and media outreach was at a critical mass. As a result, many community stakeholders understood the treachery afoot, and they weren't going to allow it to stand. I waited to resign until I could finish what I had been appointed to do: serve the needs of GLSC's constituents. Notices about the board meeting had been posted *everywhere* that week; and the board meeting was packed with students, faculty, and curious citizens—you name it, they were there. Everyone wanted to witness what was about to go down.

Right before we opened the meeting to the general public, we had a closed executive session. I quickly resigned my chair position, setting in motion my plan. On one side of the room, two Republicans started high-fiving each other. They clearly thought they'd won. On the other side of the room, an honorary board member who supported me started crying. I felt at peace with my decision because I knew what was about to hit the fan. It was straight out of *The Art of War* by Sun Tzu.

I retreated from the room, head held high, just as they opened the meeting to the public. The match had been lit, and there was no going back. As I left, I could hear people asking, "Where's the committee chair?" Those who knew what was going on behind the scenes poured into the meeting, and news of my resignation spread like wildfire. All hell broke loose in the local media. Everyone was upset about my departure—the community, the students, the union, and the faculty. It appeared that the Republicans still thought they were in control and that my resignation signaled another win for them. But their alleged malfeasance around GLSC's presidential search had already been widely and publicly exposed. They may have thought they were getting exactly what they wanted with my resignation. Instead, they were getting exactly what I believe they deserved. Importantly, none of my actions were motivated by partisanship. I was simply confronting wrongdoing to protect the university and its students. Over the years, I've registered with both parties. For me, right versus left will never trump right versus wrong.

———

I knew the presidential search would have to start over yet again—this time with a totally objective process, even without my involvement.

I also knew the politicians had shown their hand and everyone had seen it. Between the negative media attention and the entire community being up in arms, there was no way they would be able to name their guy.

GLSC's presidential search process did start over, and the school ended up finding an amazing candidate from Florida. Her tenure as the college's president has been stellar. To this day, people still thank me. Though it was tough, I would do it all over again—exactly the same way, if need be. Not only was it the right thing to do, but my choices also helped me forge strong, authentic, long-term relationships with people I could trust. Even after many years, I still treasure these friendships. The ordeal forced me to tap into new levels of courage and tenacity, and I learned so much about myself and the incredible energy you can harness when you follow your core values. It was my first experience with big government, and I was disgusted by what seemed to be entrenched corruption.

Ron supported me every step of the way—always listening, encouraging, and guiding.

"Am I doing the right thing?" I would ask him, sometimes as a whisper in the middle of a restless night.

Never annoyed, even when I'd roused him from a deep sleep, he would listen, comfort, and advise. His support was everything to me, and our marriage grew stronger as we faced this challenge together. Every life experience offers wisdom and strength for the next challenge. I knew I could get through GLSC because previous endeavors had taught me patience and stamina—marathons, Wall Street, Harvard, and more. Life experiences build on themselves. If you're still standing at the end of one challenge, then you're stronger for the next one. In my case, the years ahead would present much bigger hurdles. But anytime I'd start feeling overwhelmed, hesitant, or insecure, I'd simply stop and remind myself about what I'd already overcome. *Lori, you got through GLSC. You've got this!* With that little pep talk, I'd stand up, leave the sidelines, and jump into the fray.

You can't be a perpetual spectator. Life is played on the field, and it's when the game gets rough that you learn what you're truly capable of. You get stronger and smarter with each play. The key is to keep playing. Each of us is put here on earth for a purpose, but it's rarely discovered sitting on the sidelines. That's what I wanted my son Conner to understand that night at the dinner table so many years ago.

CHAPTER 10

There's Light at the End of Every Tunnel

"Success is 99 percent failure."

—Soichiro Honda

IN JUNE 1933, PRESIDENT FRANKLIN D. ROOSEVELT signed the Glass-Steagall Act, separating commercial and investment banks and creating the Federal Deposit Insurance Corporation (FDIC). These were protective legal measures crafted in response to the horrific financial losses of the 1929 stock market crash that set off the Great Depression. Less than a year before my fated meeting with financial con man Bernie Madoff, Glass-Steagall was repealed by Congress as part of the Financial Services Modernization Act of 1999, bringing down this protective wall and allowing banks to become substantially larger—some would later say, "too big to fail." Ironically, this 1999 legislation would put the cherry on top of the Federal Reserve Board's decision a year earlier to interpret Glass-Steagall differently and allow Citibank to merge with what was then Salomon Smith Barney. That's how the company I worked for became Citigroup Smith Barney. Needless to say, the 1990s were heady times on Wall Street. In 1996, after more than a hundred years, the Dow Jones Industrial Average (DJIA) stock market index broke 10,000 for the first time in history. Only three years later, in December 1999, stocks nearly doubled in value to 19,752. In the boom years before 9/11, Wall Street and the world of finance were on fire and changing fast.

Like many at that time, my business was thriving, but not for the same reasons as most of my colleagues. I was part of a small group of wealth advisors—a completely new breed on Wall Street. Instead of selling financial products like everyone else, we were offering research-based investing for an advisory fee based on the total value of the assets managed. At that time, my assets under management were in excess of $5.5 billion. We did everything for our clients— even walked the dog. I'm exaggerating, but not by much. To do the right thing as a wealth manager, I had to be knowledgeable, adaptive, and completely unbiased. This customer-centric, recurring-revenue model was where the financial industry would eventually gravitate. Today, three-quarters of Wall Street's business is from this type of recurring revenue. But back in the late '90s, the concept was very new, and there was plenty of resistance. Still, all of us knew that the idea of selling financial products to our high-net-worth individual and institutional clients was ludicrous. It would insult their intelligence *and* might fail to meet their needs. Everything we did was scrutinized. We were judged on our objectivity, rigor, and results. So we forged ahead, despite the roadblocks. We wanted to build relationships with our clients and provide objective, strategic advice—to do the right thing by them without all the conflicts of interest. We were definitely *not* going to feed them transaction-based financial products with hidden fees and broker incentives, like the rest of Wall

Street. As you might guess, we weren't part of the office "in" crowd. We didn't care because our clients loved what we were doing.

My work required significant human resources for research and compliance. Unfortunately, Smith Barney didn't appear willing to provide the brainpower I needed. After years of pushing, I was finally allowed to create my own research team—as long as I checked all the industry-compliance boxes and paid for things out of my own pocket. I was basically building a business within a business in order to serve my clients properly. And even though I covered the majority of my own costs, Smith Barney still took its traditional split of 40–50 percent of the income I generated. It was far from ideal.

I was becoming increasingly disillusioned with business as usual on Wall Street in the late 1990s and early 2000s. Some of us met with the leadership of Citigroup Smith Barney to help them understand our needs and consider spinning us out as a separate entity. Unfortunately, they did little more than try to placate us with hollow promises. We made a sincere effort to improve policies and processes at Smith Barney. I, for one, shared all my intellectual property and contributed to industry organizations to spread the word about what I believed was a better way of doing business. But it was increasingly clear that Smith Barney's acquisition by Citigroup had created a big bureaucracy. We were constantly fighting battles for more resources, objectivity, and people. We were becoming a smaller piece of a growing pie.

The powers in charge no longer seemed as interested in us, and it appeared that we no longer had as much clout. There was also a lot of fluctuation at the top in those days, and Citigroup was taking progressively more heat for conflicts of interests, undisclosed trading fees and incentives, and a litany of other issues that many of us had been protesting for more than a decade. We tried to make it work, but the writing was on the wall—layers of it.

During my last five years at Citigroup Smith Barney, I wasn't even buying the bank's stock anymore. We had these deferred compensation plans, and whenever I was awarded bonuses or earnouts because of my high level of production, I would put them all into cash. I also never signed any restrictive contracts. Whenever they tried to get me to sign something, I'd just say, "I'm not signing. Feel free to fire me." Of course, they never did. This meant I could leave whenever I wanted by simply following standard broker protocols. In my opinion, the conglomerate's actions were not favoring clients, and I was sick of fighting to do what I believed to be the right thing.

By August 2008, I was ready to hand in my resignation after a highly successful twenty-one-year career with Smith Barney. I'd started in the World Trade Center as a young woman in the 1980s, knowing very little about Wall Street. I was leaving as a seasoned professional with a mature team determined to practice money management the way we believed it should be practiced. My team was preparing to leave with roughly $5.5 billion in assets under management. This was achieved without ever acquiring another practice or team, or frankly, getting any referrals from colleagues or our parent company. My book of business had grown organically the old-fashioned way: through hard work, innovation, and determination.

I didn't fully realize it back then, but as part of a small band of like-minded wealth advisors, I'd help to plant seeds that would ultimately change one of the most powerful industries on the planet— an industry that was sorely in need of change, in my opinion. I was proud of the work I had done at Smith Barney, especially as one of the few women in an advisory role there. But it was time to say goodbye to a business model I no longer believed in and start a new chapter of my career as an independent financial advisor. At the time, we were the biggest team to ever exit a large full-service brokerage firm.

As part of Smith Barney's branch system, I had spent the last twenty or so years working in Rochester, where Ron and I had decided to raise our two sons. I was one of the biggest producers in the region, even though none of my business was local. Still, when I decided to leave, I had to resign to David Smith, the head of our small branch office. David had actually been one of my training managers in the World Trade Center when I started my career. I liked and respected him. Because I was bringing in a lot of revenue, I knew my resignation would deeply impact him as well as the overall health and morale of the branch. It was a conversation I was dreading, but the time had come.

I knocked on his open door reluctantly and walked into his office. He looked up from the paperwork on his desk with a casual smile. "Hi, Lori. Come in. What's up?"

"David, I'm sorry that I have to do this, but . . ."

He went pale before I could finish my sentence. "Well, it isn't like you didn't try to tell me, Lori." He was aware that I'd had numerous meetings with the CEO of Smith Barney as well as all the way up and down the Citigroup leadership team.

"You know I've been trying to make this work for a long time, David. But things just aren't changing. It's time for me to go."

He nodded somberly. I walked over and gave him a big hug. Then I packed up, got in my car, and drove across town to the new office I'd set up just before the transition. It was time to start calling my clients and share the news. I could have taken my lucrative book of business to another large brokerage like Merrill Lynch—and received a huge check for doing so. But I chose a different path, one that aligned with my personal and professional values and goals. Becoming an independent advisor was the road less traveled. In fact, back then, it was the road *not* traveled—there were so few of us in the beginning. But it would allow me to continue serving my clients in the customer-centric, transparent way that I believed in. Making such a big leap felt overwhelming at that point in my career. I was ready to go independent, but not yet ready to hang my own shingle. I lacked the technology infrastructure and platform to serve my sophisticated client base. So I sought out an established independent advisory firm with which to partner. My choice was Brimstone Capital Advisors—a choice I would soon regret. But during those first days as an independent, I thought I was in good hands.

After handing in my resignation to David, the rest of the day went smoothly. But the next morning, Citigroup placed a temporary restraining order (TRO) on me. Luckily, this was overturned quickly because my team and I had followed broker protocols to the letter. I had taken nothing other than client names and phone numbers. I'd even left my artwork hanging on the wall. Generally, when the courts throw out a TRO that fast, it means the complainant does not have a case. It was an encouraging sign that Citigroup was unlikely to sue. But I was wrong.

"Oh my God!" I said aloud, sitting alone in my new office only a week later. It was Thursday, September 4, 2008, and I was staring at a summons from Citigroup on my desk. They were suing me and asking for millions in damages. The lawsuit claimed breach of contract, conversion/fraud, breach of fiduciary duty, misappropriation of trade secrets, intentional interference with business relationships, unfair competition, civil conspiracy, and raiding.

I took a deep breath and immediately retained a well-known, expensive law firm. I knew I needed the best if I was going to take on a Goliath like Citigroup. The lawyers went through everything with me, and we immediately denied all allegations. My counterclaim asserted tortious interference with economic relations, unfair competition, defamation, injurious falsehood, and failure to comply with the protocol for broker recruiting and Financial Industry Regulatory Authority (FINRA) rules.

After the initial shock wore off, I was indignant. "How dare they? For what? I didn't do anything wrong," I told my lawyer and colleagues in the new firm, all of whom had come with me from Citigroup. "All I did was give away my intellectual property for years and teach other advisors to be more effective. I gave my work to everybody. I paid my own bills, for God's sake! Smith Barney never referred me clients. How *dare* they!"

"You're not an indentured servant," my lawyer agreed. "They don't have a case."

It was encouraging to hear, but he wasn't done. "Lori, you know if this doesn't settle, it will go to arbitration, and that carries big risks, especially for the little guy. You could end up splitting the baby or worse."

I stood up and started pacing the room. "Are you freaking kidding me?"

But I'd watched other cases unfold and knew he was right. According to FINRA, 69 percent of these kinds of cases settle. Only 18 percent go to arbitration. History favored a settlement. I knew I'd have to write a multimillion-dollar check and pay big legal fees, even though I'd done nothing wrong. It was completely unjust, but settling was my best option—the lesser of two evils. I needed to wrap this up and move on.

This was not the only trouble brewing in my world. In fact, 2008 and 2009 would become some of the most trying years of my life. Only eleven days after I had received the summons from Citigroup, Lehman Brothers filed bankruptcy, and Merrill Lynch collapsed as part of the subprime mortgage meltdown that had begun in 2007. The breakdown of these enormous investment banks and financial firms caused stocks and commodities to plummet worldwide on September 15, 2008. The chaos continued during the week of October 6, with the US markets continuing to close lower five days in a row. Trading volume was record-breaking as the DJIA fell more than 1,874 points—18 percent—its worst weekly decline ever. Standard & Poor's 500 Index fell more than 20 percent. By October 11, the head of the International Monetary Fund (IMF), Dominique Strauss-Kahn of France, warned that the world financial system was teetering on the "brink of systemic meltdown."

A couple of weeks later, on October 24, 2008, many of the world's stock exchanges experienced the worst daily declines in their history. The deputy governor of the Bank of England, Charlie Bean, called the situation "possibly the largest financial crisis of its kind in human history." The declines continued for another six months, with the DJIA finally hitting bottom on March 6, 2009, having dropped 54 percent to 6,469 from a high of 14,164 on October 9, 2007.

It was a terrifying roller-coaster ride and clearly a terrible time to go independent. But that's exactly what I had done. Behind the scenes, my departure from Citigroup had been busy and chaotic, with a lot of planning on top of my normal workload. I'd never sold or merged with a company before, so I'd hired someone to help me find the right firm and deal structure. Through this process, I was introduced to Alan Brynstan, Brimstone's charismatic, ambitious CEO. He, and his number two guy, Paul Swagger, wanted to be the biggest of the nation's independent advisory firms. Our first meeting was at their sleek East Coast office. It didn't look anything like a typical, stodgy bank meeting venue. I remember the space's chic design and hip artwork. It was impressive and looked like the place printed money. Alan confidently entered the room.

"Lori, great to finally meet you in person. Make yourself comfortable. Would you like some coffee, tea, sparkling water? Something to eat after your trip?" He opened up a hidden wall cabinet filled with high-end snacks. "I'm sorry Paul can't join us today."

"Thank you, Alan. Some water would be great." I was immediately impressed by his charm and command of the room. He asked me a few questions and let his accomplishments flow. *He's done these dog and pony shows before,* I thought. But I was listening. He'd come highly recommended, and I respected his confidence. I nodded to continue as a screen dropped slowly from the ceiling and Alan started his presentation. It was stylish and unexpected. I was looking for something different than what Alan was delivering. The numbers on the screen were almost too good to be true. He made it clear that if we could come to terms, I would be getting in on the ground floor of something big.

After many months of due diligence, I took a few more weeks to consider Alan's offer. We had been thorough, but when we tried to dig deeper, they pushed back—and we yielded. We compromised on terms and full transparency. The night before we signed, I had a sick feeling. I questioned whether I was doing the right thing. There had been significant back-and-forth, lots of negotiating, and many points of frustration. The next morning, I shook off my concerns, signed the paperwork, and alerted my team about what to expect next.

As a stressed-out first-timer, I'd relied on the numbers and information as it was presented. I'd wanted out of Citigroup Smith Barney, so I gave in to both wishful thinking and deal fatigue. It was the worst professional mistake of my life. I did exactly what I *did not* do with Madoff: I fell for the window dressing. I prided myself on my diligence skills, problem-solving abilities, and out-of-network perspective when protecting my clients. But this time, I let myself be pulled into a bad situation.

The revenue numbers Alan had presented to me in our first meeting never materialized. The closer I looked, the more it seemed like they were double-dipping. I just hadn't seen it at first. Because I would never misrepresent my numbers, I wanted to believe Brimstone would never misrepresent theirs. From what I could see, Alan and his team appeared to be getting paid fees for financial products while taking quarterly or monthly advisory fees as well. This was exactly what I'd fought against during my entire career at Smith Barney. Yet here I was, hanging my hat with a firm that appeared to be doing what I loathed—and it was too late. I hadn't stress tested Brimstone's numbers enough. I should have slowed down the process and hired a forensic auditor, but I hadn't. I also hadn't taken the time to study their culture. I hadn't fully explored the value system of their leadership team. I should have looked at previous transactions and employee turnover. The reality was, I'd cut corners, and it was coming back to bite me in the ass.

Alan and his team had made it seem like I was the one making out in our deal, but it's more likely that Brimstone wanted *my* team's national brand and reputation—the one we'd spent so many years building at Smith Barney. They wanted to get into the national rankings, and we were their ticket. My goal had been to move my business so I could do right by my clients. I wanted to be independent. I felt that someday large brokerages would no longer dominate the industry. But I'd made a huge mistake hitching my wagon to

Brimstone. I'd been seeking processes and technology infrastructure to ensure solid research and legal compliance for my team, but what Alan and his team were offering turned out to be Swiss cheese—holes everywhere!

I kept thinking things would fall into place once I got settled, but they never did. The global financial crisis that was unfolding all around us quickly revealed Brimstone's flaws. The firm was under-resourced. They were losing tons of clients and revenue. Even some of my clients were leaving because of Brimstone's missteps.

"Lori, we love you and we love your team," I had one departing client tell me. "But you got in bed with the devil."

Within a few months, my book of business was one of the biggest revenue streams supporting Brimstone. They were even able to get into the national rankings and initially mask their problems because of the added assets and revenue we brought in. Despite saving their asses, we'd never see any earn-outs because the market had dropped so much. I knew I'd made a terrible mistake, but Brimstone had outlawyered me with restrictive covenants, and I couldn't get out.

As I sat at my desk poring over their dismal financials, I thought, *Oh my God, what have I done?*

I'd spent decades building a stellar professional reputation. It was why clients came to me and stayed with me. My reputation was my business. And sitting there looking at the numbers that day, I felt physically ill. Brimstone appeared to be in shambles. The markets were in turmoil. And Citigroup was not settling. I was in deep trouble, and I had to tell my husband.

"Ron," I began over dinner that night, "I'm in league with some people whom I believe to be very bad, and I'm worried I'll never be able to clear my name."

He placed his hand on mine across the table and gave it a gentle squeeze.

I took a liberal sip of my cabernet and looked him in the eyes. "And I have to say this out loud: We might lose everything. We might go bankrupt. Between Citigroup, the dismal state of the markets, and Brimstone, we could lose everything. The Brimstone team seems toxic, and I'm linked to them . . . and it's all my fault."

"Lori, just stay calm. We'll get through this. Take a deep breath. It's all going to be okay."

But I couldn't calm my nerves. I was sick, thinking about all the people depending on me. "What will my team do—and their families? What will my mom do and . . . what about my clients?!" I started sobbing.

I kept thinking, *I've been hoodwinked, and all these innocent people are going to suffer for my mistake.* I kept wondering, *How could I have been so blind to all of Brimstone's problems?* I wanted to crawl under a rock and hide, but I knew I had to fight on—if not to save myself, at least to save everyone else.

For many months, Brimstone continued its nosedive. Every day, they lost more fees and revenue, a problem that was magnified by what I believed to be double-dipping. It was excruciating. I would wake up and wonder how I was going to face another sixteen-hour day filled with anger, despair, stress, and chaos. It was depressing, debilitating, and humiliating. I was still battling Citigroup while trying to keep my head above water at Brimstone. In the end, a closely held bank that was a minority owner in Brimstone bought up the shares and became the majority owner, providing a temporary bailout. Alan, true to form, seemed unrepentant.

"This is not what I signed up for, Alan," I snapped, not even trying to hide my animosity toward him anymore. "This is my life's work."

As I remember it, he shrugged and said, "You'll get used to it, Lori. You're a bank employee now, just like me."

"No, I won't. I will never get used to this." I turned and stormed away. To me, it looked like he'd built a house of cards for his own financial gain and didn't give a damn about who he hurt along the way.

After nearly eighteen months, Citigroup Global Markets Inc. (CGMI) and its subsidiary Smith Barney pushed the case into arbitration. They were clearly trying to make an example out of me. But ultimately, after considering all the pleadings, testimony, and evidence presented, the arbitration panel dismissed Citigroup's Statement of Claim with prejudice. My counterclaims—and those of my colleagues who had also been sued—were likewise dismissed. All requests for attorney's fees were denied, although Citigroup had to pay $38,000 in session fees to the courts. I had won. It had taken almost two years and $1 million in legal fees, but I had beaten Goliath.

After the FINRA panel dismissed all claims and requests with prejudice, securities industry lawyer Bill Singer commented on the case in a May 7, 2010, blog post called, "Citigroup Is Dunne-In by FINRA Arbitration Loss":

> Although all claims of all parties were dismissed, this was clearly a big black eye of a loss of Citigroup/ Smith Barney.
>
> As I have often said about these "send 'em a message" cases, very often the message gets lost in the mail… [A] firm such as CGMI has this one major Achille's Heel: It can't afford to lose a single arbitration. When CGMI loses a case, such as this one, it becomes part of the lore of Wall Street. Which means that brokers gather round the water coolers, at the bar on Friday afternoon, and on the online forums and talk about how so-and-so spit in CGMI's face and got away with it—*and if I ever decide to leave, I'm not taking any crap from them either!*

After the Citigroup lawsuit concluded in my favor, it was time to get out of the corner I'd painted myself into at Brimstone. In the end, I agreed to pay the bank that purchased Brimstone $2 million for a clean break and to release me from all restrictions. Yep, after all I'd been through, I paid them! I knew the bank had no idea they'd acquired a failed organization in Brimstone. I also knew things would get worse soon, so I cut my losses and ran. In the end, the bank was sold to a larger institution, and Brimstone folded with stakeholders selling off the nearly worthless remnants, trying to recoup some of their losses. I was glad to have been spared those tortuous final days and to have walked away, miraculously with my reputation still intact.

In October 2011, I formed LVW Advisors, my own independent financial advisory firm. I was finally back on my feet, though definitely still smarting. I did a complete postmortem on everything that had happened. I was determined to get everything right with my own firm but was still reliving and talking about my Brimstone mistakes almost every day. I was stuck in a state of regret, and it was eating away at my confidence. At dinner one evening, my dear friend Chris Poch said to me, "Lori, stop beating yourself up. You were green. You made mistakes. You didn't know. You weren't as smart as you are now."

It was a great lesson. You can't rewrite history and leave out the parts you don't like, but you can't get stuck in the past, either. One of the biggest takeaways from that time in my life was to own my mistakes, grow from them, and move on. Despite all the pain, I had learned a lot from the Brimstone debacle. These hard-won lessons would strengthen me both personally and professionally. I was a better businessperson and advisor for the experience. Adversity is, as ever, a great teacher if you allow it to be.

In 2012, only a year after I'd opened LVW Advisors, I was invited to an important industry cocktail party atop the Bellagio Hotel in Las Vegas. When the elevator doors opened on the second floor of the thirty-six-story building, in stepped Representative Barney Frank of Massachusetts. As coauthor of the 2010 Dodd-Frank Wall Street reform law, Frank had been asked by many of his fellow

Democrats to reinstate Glass-Steagall and restore the protective barrier between commercial and investment banks. Representative Frank saw things differently and chose not to support a reversal of the repeal of Glass-Steagall. Many progressives on Capitol Hill felt that the repeal of Glass-Steagall in 1999 had laid the foundation for the global financial crash of 2008. Whether true or not, the irony of seeing Representative Frank at this event did not fully hit me until 2015 when I read in *The Wall Street Journal* that he had been elected to the board of directors of Signature Bank in New York. I shook my head and thought, *What a very small world.* The memory would take on even greater significance when Signature Bank was seized by regulators on March 12, 2023.

As I got off the elevator and entered the opulent penthouse alongside Representative Frank, my stomach turned. Across the room, directly in front of me, was Alan. After Brimstone's slow, public, lawyer-filled spiral to rock bottom, Alan had moved on. The mounting regulatory and legal proceedings seemed to have weighed more heavily on Alan's partner, Paul, who had taken his life in the middle of the debacle. It was heartbreaking, no matter the circumstances. I took a deep breath and a moment to ponder my next move. The best course of action, I decided, was *not* to avoid Alan. It was time. I'd finally moved on, and all my anger toward Alan and Brimstone had shifted. Now, I could only think about the monumental tragedy of it all. What a waste!

I walked over to the small group gathered around him. *How can he possible show his face here,* I wondered? To me, he seemed to burn every bridge he'd ever crossed, then simply reinvent himself. I thought he was the embodiment of narcissism.

"Lori." He smiled stiffly and leaned in for an obligatory cheek kiss, undoubtedly trying to hide his nerves upon seeing me. "It's *so* good to see you."

I also forced a smile and thought, *Here he is in an expensive penthouse suite, enjoying cocktails like nothing has happened.* He'd cost my business billions and put me and my team through years of hell.

Okay, maybe I hadn't completely moved on, but I was in a much better place and certainly wasn't going to let him have the last word.

"Terrible news about Paul, isn't it, Lori? I'm sure you've heard." Alan shook his head.

"Yes, it's a tragedy. It's *all* such a terrible tragedy, Alan." I spoke slowly, emphasizing each word. There was a moment of silence. I hoped he understood the subtext.

"Yes, a tragedy," he responded, seeming to look around to see how others were reading the conversation.

Of course, he didn't get my subtext, I thought.

I leaned in with a half smile. "Al, you know, I have to thank you."

"Really?" His smile reappeared, his surprise seeming earnest.

"Yes, really, I do. I mean, I've built a much stronger advisory firm as a result of living through all the mistakes I witnessed at Brimstone." Though I can't deny I was enjoying the awkwardness of the moment, I actually meant this sincerely. I'd survived the hell of that experience and learned what *not* to do.

Alan's smile faded, but he held my gaze. "Ah . . . well . . . that's good."

I admit, it was really nice to see his silver tongue go mute for once.

CHAPTER 11

Values and Accountability Matter

*"When values, thoughts, feelings, and actions
are in alignment, person becomes focused,
and character is strengthened."*

—John C. Maxwell

THERE WERE QUITE A FEW HEADLINES IN THE
news after I formed LVW Advisors, like this one in the March 21,
2012, issue of *Forbes*: "Going Independent: Wirehouse Superstar
Goes Solo." Wirehouse is a nickname for a full-service investment
bank/broker-dealer. A special report in the *Financial Times* on June
17, 2015, captured the wider shift we had set in motion: "Wirehouses
in Decline as Advisers Seek Independence." It referenced my group's
2008 departure from Smith Barney:

> The high-profile exits of a $5bn group led by Lori
> Van Dusen from Smith Barney, and a nearly $1bn
> team of four Merrill Lynch veterans (who formed
> LLBH Private Wealth Management) were most no-
> table for where they went: to the independent chan-
> nel. And they led a flurry in the years since, not only
> of wirehouse advisors going independent but also of
> platforms launching to support these breakaways.

It is rewarding to know that I helped launch a movement. Though it was a lonely, bumpy road to walk for so many years, I was proud to contribute to the change I thought the financial industry so desperately needed. But after the Brimstone debacle, I had to rebuild my company, my confidence, and my life.

Whatever I'd seen done at Brimstone I avoided at LVW Advisors. Where Brimstone lacked a strong culture, LVW would be closely aligned with my personal and professional values of integrity, honesty, respect, compassion, and a commitment to serving others. We have stayed true to our promise to put our clients' needs first. I was recently contacted by a veteran consultant and professional investor who told me he was struck by LVW's unique approach. He commented on the firm's thoughtful, proactive team, customized thinking, problem solving, and solutions. It was great to hear this from an industry expert because, for me, starting LVW was about treating our clients well, earning their trust, and managing their assets in their best interest. People will always come first at LVW—both our clients and our team. Many of the people at LVW have been working with me for decades. As we continue to grow, we all spend a lot of time finding, mentoring, and training the right people who share our values and are willing to work hard on behalf of our clients. *This* is what really matters, and I wouldn't have it any other way.

In a sermon I heard many years ago, the pastor said, "Money only makes you more of what you already are."

It's true. Money is simply money. It's spiritually neutral. It's not the ticket to happiness or the root of all evil. This popular expression is a common misquote of the Bible verse from 1 Timothy, which reads: "For *the love of money* is the root of all evil: which while some *coveted* after, they have erred from the faith, and pierced themselves through with many sorrows." Having money and coveting money are two very different things. Right now, I have enough money, but I don't covet it. Having navigated many market crashes and the Brimstone debacle, I've seen how fleeting money can be. It comes and it goes. Money can be a wonderful tool, but it's an unreliable measure of worth.

As you can imagine, I meet a lot of people with a lot of money in my line of work. Those who measure their value or happiness by the money they accumulate often cause themselves and others a great deal of misery and damage. Those who hoard their money, wield it over others, and believe it buys them some sort of status make a big mistake. Those who use their money to do good do the most amazing and wonderful things. Money behind a noble mission can change the world for the better.

Given that I'm a wealth advisor, it may seem ironic, but my career has never been about the money. For me, it's personal. When people share their financial circumstances, they're sharing much more than just dollars and cents. They're confiding in me about their successes and failures, their hopes and dreams. It's a responsibility I don't take lightly. Yes, I am blessed to be able to live the American dream and am very grateful for the life financial success has afforded my family and me. But I find fulfillment in strong relationships with good people. Everything else flows from this. We deliver excellent outcomes for our clients because we never forget that we serve human beings who have entrusted us with their life stories and wealth, which are always about much more than just money.

Anyone who has founded their own company knows how much work is involved. It's invigorating, but exhausting. There aren't enough hours in the day to get everything done. It's even more grueling for parents. When a founder goes home after a long day at work, they still have to rally enough mental and emotional energy to truly be there for their kids and spouse. It's a tough balancing act, but I believe it's worth the extra effort.

Being Conner and Cole's mom has been the greatest joy and honor of my life. When Conner was born, I made a vow that I would be there for my children. I made sure the cookies and brownies were delivered for the fundraisers and class festivities, even if they weren't homemade (I love to cook but don't bake). I was there to cheer them on from the bleachers, even if that meant running like a madwoman in heels and a suit across a mushy field to make it to the start of a game. Nights and weekends were all about family, even when I was wiped out from a tough week. I leaned and relied heavily on my husband, who was a great support.

Family dinners were a priority. Though it could be challenging to get everyone to the table at the same time, we made it happen most nights. Ron would go to the store and prep things in the kitchen. I'd rush home and cook everything up. On busy weekdays, meals were simple—roast chicken, pork chops, or fish with a side of grilled veggies and rice. The food wasn't anything fancy, but it was healthy and balanced. More important, dinner brought us together to talk about our days. On the weekends, I enjoyed cooking up a big Italian meal or something creative, and often invited my mom, extended family, and close friends to join us.

As I built a successful business on my own terms, I was able to work from home more often. I definitely had to put in the hours, but not in a traditional nine-to-five structure. Odd hours were the norm, so I could make time for my kids during the day. If I wanted to leave work early to watch one of my boys play in a soccer game in the afternoon, I'd work for an hour or two after they went to bed. In the end, the work got done. I was busy but happy. As my business grew, my flexibility also grew. This became foundational for my success.

Nontraditional work hours were rare for people in my field at that time. Today, with the more widespread acceptance of remote work and flexible hours, many people are opting for more work-life balance. I was just lucky enough to do this before it became mainstream. This kept my world whole, so I didn't burn out as the pressures of a thriving business grew. Many successful women know that flexibility matters and there is more than one way to do things. Instead of fixating on the trodden path to success, often it's better to do what's right for your well-being and that of those you love. My experience showed me how this approach pays back in multiples.

Even before I founded LVW Advisors, I had learned how to set limits in order to be the mom and wife I wanted to be. It was not uncommon for me to say, "I can't do that," or "I won't be able to make that meeting." I was criticized for it, especially in the beginning of my career when there were no women in my industry, and none of the men around me understood anything about the stress of being a working mother. Luckily, in my profession, the numbers were what mattered. As a top producer, it was more important for me to serve my clients than attend meetings. I was always comfortable saying, "Sorry, I can't make that meeting. You can fire me." Honestly, I invited people to fire me a lot. If I couldn't enjoy my family, what did it matter anyway? That was my thinking.

I had a lot of interactions with male professionals with spouses at home. Many of these men loved their kids but did not have to worry about them. I was very protective of my family time and fought hard to preserve it. That's not to say that there weren't tough choices. I worked a lot of hours. I didn't have time for much else besides work and family when my kids were young. I had to prioritize. And let's be honest, when priorities conflict, the quality of work can suffer. It happens. Sometimes you just do a crappy job. Your head is not in the game because of something going on in your personal life. You have to be honest with yourself and accept that you're not at the top of your game. When you can, make things right. If you are honest with people, they will understand.

A reputation of excellence certainly helps in these times. I worked all hours to serve my clients—early mornings, late nights, and weekends. It was intense, but I'm not telling a working mother or female entrepreneur anything she hasn't experienced. It's a tough juggling act, and you have to check in with yourself from time to time and ask, *How am I feeling? Am I tired? What do I need to do to bring life back into balance?* Mental, spiritual, and physical well-being must be maintained so things don't spiral out of control. Even today, if I'm going off the rails and the stress becomes all-consuming, I step away and do what's necessary to find my balance. I meditate, go for a long run, and rejuvenate. I come back when I feel ready. If I'm trying to spend time with my family, write something meaningful, think about a problem deeply, analyze market trends, or meditate, I walk away from technology. My phone goes on "Do Not Disturb." I try to be intentional about carving out quiet time to think and be. This is much more important, and challenging, in today's hyper-connected world.

I was also lucky enough to be able to afford quality childcare during the day. There are a lot of people in this country who cannot afford help. It's a huge crisis that must be addressed. Eventually, I was at a point where I was successful enough to push back and demand change, like I did at Smith Barney. But it took time. Later, as an entrepreneur, I was able to create change for at least some working mothers, which was very rewarding.

———

I couldn't have achieved all that I have without my husband, Ron. He made it possible for me to nurture a healthy business and happy family. Ron was an amazing father and supportive husband. Not only did he coach our boys, but he also coached and positively influenced many young men in our community through baseball, football, soccer, wrestling, and more. He kept himself in great shape and never asked a kid to do something he wouldn't do himself. He could outrun most of the boys during conditioning drills. Sometimes, to prove a point, he'd have the boys run up a hill while he did so backward. Then he would pass them and meet them at the top. Ron modeled what he expected of his players, and made them better people, one practice at a time.

My husband's childhood was far from idyllic. His dad never made his son's games. Instead, he drank and beat Ron's mother. It wasn't something my husband ever wanted to talk about. He buried the difficult memories of trying to protect his mother from harm. For his entire life, he battled depression, tried to stuff down the anger and sadness, and quietly fought the many demons of his stolen childhood. He tried to overcome his past by working on himself and reading the Bible daily. But he was a proud man and would not seek the professional help he needed, despite my constant encouragement. Instead, he poured himself into fatherhood to make sure his boys had the devoted father and idyllic life he'd never experienced. Ron did everything with great passion and in service to others. I see him in our boys now, and it makes me so proud.

We worked hard to raise good boys, despite our own baggage and imperfections. We wanted our sons to know that as men they could be both kind and strong, because these two qualities sit so beautifully side by side. I saw both of these characteristics in my grandfather. When I was little, I always felt that I could talk to him about anything. When I went to college in Ithaca, New York, he would just show up out of the blue sometimes to visit. There was no way for me to know that he was coming because there were no cell phones. So he would just show up, and I would be so happy when I saw him. We had a tight bond, and I have benefited greatly from his wisdom. He understood that it was his job to nurture me and then let me go.

Ron and I tried to do the same with our boys, avoiding the helicopter and bulldozer parenting prevalent in our wealthy, entitled community. Our children would always be held accountable for their behavior. It wasn't easy, and sometimes we had to get creative. For example, when my younger son, Cole, was three years old, he developed a terrible habit of giving everyone raspberries and biting them when he did not get his way. I read all the parenting books to try to stop this behavior. I tried serious face-to-face discussions, time-outs, taking away his treasured toys (he was obsessed with toy cars)—you name it. Nothing worked.

I was at the end of my rope when I picked him up from preschool one day and the teacher told me he had bitten a classmate. I remembered an operant conditioning experiment I'd seen when I was a teacher's assistant in the psychology rat lab in college. *Truly unconventional,* I thought, *but what do I have to lose?* When Cole tried to bite his brother the next day, I picked him up and brought him to the kitchen. I sat him at the dinner table, opened the refrigerator, and took out a bottle of Tabasco sauce. Placing the smallest possible dab on his tongue, I said, "No more biting, Cole!" As the hot sauce hit his mouth, he screamed and cried. It was quite dramatic. But from then on, I simply showed him the bottle if he was trying to bite anyone. The mere suggestion of hot sauce compelled him to stop. It was certainly not perfect parenting, but I'm still glad I did it. It worked. And guess what? Today, Cole loves superhot sauce. So maybe he wasn't completely scarred by the experience after all.

My older son, Conner, had his moments, too. When he was a new driver in his late teens, he often broke the speed limit. My daily mantra was, "Do not speed, Conner." One blustery October night when he was eighteen comes to mind as a night my overconfident teen did not listen. It was rutting season, and I knew a lot of deer, especially big bucks, were actively running out of the woods and across the roads. I was petrified that Conner would hit a buck with his foot on the accelerator, which could be deadly. He pulled out of the driveway, and I decided to follow him. He had no idea. As I expected, Conner began to speed. Within a few minutes, he was pulled over by a local sheriff. "Thank goodness,"

I said out loud in my car. I pulled over behind them and started to get out of my car.

"Ma'am," the sheriff called out, "please stay in your car."

"That is my son, and you'd better give him a ticket!" I called back. The sheriff nodded, and I complied with his request.

Once he'd finished with Conner, he walked back to my car. I rolled down the window.

"I left him with a warning, ma'am." He smiled. "I figured his punishment at home was going to be more than any ticket I could give him."

I laughed and thanked the officer, even though I secretly wished he'd fined my son. It would have been the perfect natural consequence for speeding. Nevertheless, being pulled over had the right effect. Conner was extremely shaken. And the officer was right: when we returned home, I confiscated my son's car keys.

Because of the work I do, I often get asked about the role of wealth in parenting and family dynamics. As I've mentioned, money itself is neutral—nothing more than a tool for good or evil. Unfortunately, I've seen a lot of "deep pockets" parenting—buying children things to promote appropriate behavior. It rarely works, and over time can be quite destructive. I'm not a fan of papering over problems with money. Many years ago, one of my clients nicely articulated the long-term problem with this approach: "Small kids, small problems. Big kids, big problems."

As a working mom, trying my best to balance work and family, I was an anomaly in my affluent community. Most of the other women were full-time moms. I couldn't help but notice the occasional sideways glances as I huffed and puffed my way into the stands after running in heels from a meeting. My daily balancing act definitely had its highs and lows. In 2005, a high: I was honored to receive the March of Dimes "Mother of the Year" award from the local

Rochester chapter. That same year, a low: I hired a criminal to watch my kids. Yep, true story, and not a particularly proud mother-of-the-year moment.

You may be wondering whether I ran a background check. I did. I was even introduced to her through a reputable agency, but nothing is foolproof. Luckily, she only worked for us for about a month. I noticed a few things had gone missing from the house, and our dry cleaner called me personally to let me know that the sitter had left Cole, my ten-year-old troublemaker, alone in the car right next to a very busy street. Two years later, Cole was watching the morning news as Ron made him breakfast before school, and there she was, arrested for grand larceny!

Cole absolutely despised the woman for the short month she nannied him. But considering he didn't have the best track record with caretakers, we didn't exactly believe every story he told us. To have the boy-who-cried-wolf situation turn into a true wolf situation was a big deal. Trust me, I still have not heard the end of it. Needless to say, it was a humbling reminder that even with the best intentions, moms make mistakes.

CHAPTER 12

We Are So Much More Than Our DNA

"The only person you are destined to become is the person you decide to be."

—*Ralph Waldo Emerson*

MY PERSONAL TIES TO THE SOUTHERN TIP OF Manhattan run even deeper than my professional ones. Way back in 1624, when the colony of New Netherland was established by the Dutch West India Company, a successful settlement was set up at the bottom tip of the island, then known as "Manatus." Christened New Amsterdam, this was the settlement where my ancestor Abraham Pietersen van Deusen stepped off the boat from Holland nearly four hundred years ago. He was referred to as Abraham the Miller, and his descendants took on the surname Van Dusen with a number of variations—Van

Deusen, Van Deursen, Van Duzer, and so forth. Among the first few hundred settlers in Manhattan, Abraham ran a windmill where Dutch grain was ground. From these humble beginnings, he now boasts some two hundred thousand descendants, across fifteen generations, scattered throughout the Americas. I am one of them.

For history buffs, my family tree is quite fascinating. Not only was Abraham, as one article put it, "the patriarch to one of the original New York dynasties," but he also participated in one of the first public councils in the New World—a precursor of the democracy that America was to become. Presidents Martin Van Buren and Franklin Delano Roosevelt are both descendants of Abraham Pietersen van Deusen. The *New York Times* did a whole piece on the family's history in July of 2011, "The Van Dusens of New Amsterdam." I remember reading it and thinking, *Pretty illustrious pedigree, if you're into that sort of thing.*

Personally, my relationship with my Van Dusen lineage has always been strained. I decided to reach out to my biological father, Jack Van Dusen, for the first time when I was twenty-four years old, just after I had graduated from Harvard. I wasn't looking to fill some void. I'd had a great childhood despite never knowing my biological father. I was simply curious. *Who is this man that no one in my family speaks about—this man who left us when we were babies?*

When I told my mom I was going to contact my father, she was upset. "I always knew you would do this, Lori!"

I sent Jack Van Dusen a letter, but it was his wife, Gloria, who called me back. "Jack wants to meet you. He has struggled with this his whole life." To my surprise, he still lived nearby in Rochester, so he came and picked me up for lunch in his big white Cadillac a few days later.

From the get-go our meeting was odd and strained. Being a modern, young professional, I pushed open the door to the restaurant on my own. This apparently displeased Jack.

"Geez, what are you, a feminist?" he mumbled. "I wanted to get the door for you."

I pretended not to hear him, but his snipe didn't make a good impression. We sat down at a table in the middle of Pittsford's historic Spring House restaurant, and Jack immediately ordered his first martini. It was noon on a Tuesday. I learned he was a line worker at the Rochester General Motors plant. He asked me what I did, and I told him about my graduation from Harvard and my forthcoming position at Shearson Lehman Brothers.

"*Mmmph.* I thought the boy would do something like that," he shrugged, referring to my brother, Scott, who had absolutely no interest in having anything to do with his biological father.

We were only five minutes into lunch, but I was already checking out. As Jack's martinis flowed, his tongue loosened. He started telling me that my grandfather's "strong personality" was to blame for him not taking a more active role in his children's lives.

Wow, I remember thinking, *that's a lame excuse. How dare he blame Grandpa. Get me out of here!*

By the end of our one-hour lunch, Jack was three martinis in and had shared a good number of his life regrets. On the outside I listened politely, but inside I just kept thinking, *Thank God this man didn't raise me!* After a final round of small talk—and Jack's final slug of alcohol—we drove home. I couldn't wait to get out of the car. I said goodbye quickly, shook his hand awkwardly, and we went our separate ways. Except for a quick drop-in to deliver a baby gift when my son Conner was born, our lunch at Spring House was the last time I really saw my biological father.

Jack Van Dusen was nothing more than a sperm donor in my life. I had come to terms with this fact a long time ago. They say the opposite of love is not hate but indifference. That's what I felt for a long time—indifference. I've since forgiven my father, but after our brief encounter, I knew just how lucky I was to be raised by my grandparents. Out of respect, I never told them about my lunch at the Spring House restaurant. They would have been sad.

In July 2016, I received a call at my offices in Rochester. My assistant patched it through.

"It's a lawyer, Lori. He says it's about Jack Van Dusen."

I picked up the line but already knew my father was dead. On the other end was a man who said he was not only Jack's lawyer but also his neighbor in Naples, Florida. Apparently, Jack and Gloria had retired there. He explained that Jack had died of cancer on Tuesday, August 1, and Gloria had passed of natural causes the next day. They were both in their eighties.

"Ms. Van Dusen," the lawyer said matter-of-factly, "they have each left a third of their estate to your mother."

The lawyer rolled off a list of Jack and Gloria's assets and calculated that my mother would receive around $300,000.

That's a fair amount of guilt, I thought. *He must have had a lot of regrets.*

I wondered if Gloria had passed on the money on her own or because my father had pressured her into doing so. Either way, we'd never know.

I also didn't know which odd piece of news to react to first. *Jack and Gloria both died within twenty-four hours of each other? I'm the one who has to tell my mom that her ex-husband, who abandoned her with two babies, has now left her money—along with his wife? Really?* I wondered if I should feel some sense of grief or loss. To be honest, in my job, I knew what was involved in settling an estate, so I mostly just felt exhausted thinking about all the work ahead to sort this all out.

With few options, I took a big slurp of coffee and walked down the hall to see my mom. She had been working with me for many years, and I found her bent over her big desk shuffling through papers.

"Hi, Mom." I motioned for her to take a break and sit down. "I have to talk to you about something."

She kept shuffling.

"Mom, I have some pretty big news to share. I think you should sit down."

She rolled her eyes in my direction. "I'm busy."

I politely but firmly motioned again for her to sit down in her chair.

She crossed her arms and plopped down like a child being put in time-out.

"Mom," I paused, then blurted out, "Jack died."

"So?" She shrugged. She didn't even blink. It was if I'd just told her it was going to rain—no emotion whatsoever.

I continued undeterred. "I think he had cancer, but I haven't talked to him in years."

She shrugged again, ready to get back to work.

"His wife, Gloria, died twenty-four hours later." Again, her facial expression showed only indifference.

"Was she sick?" my mom asked.

"I don't know, Mom, but they both left you a third of their combined estate."

Her expression shifted as she leaned forward, her eyes widening. "No, they didn't!"

"Mom, seriously, why would I make this up? It's about three hundred thousand dollars." We were both silent for a moment, trying to process the odd and unexpected news.

As if snapping out of a trance, she threw herself backward in the chair and said, "Well, it's about time. He never paid me a dime of child support."

———

A few days later, Ron and I flew down to Florida to meet the attorney and help get things in order. Jack and Gloria's house needed to be cleaned out. Jack's car had to be sold. There were pensions and plenty of paperwork to sort through. Their house was dark and musty, but everything appeared to be in good order, especially the paperwork. True to his Van Dusen heritage, Jack seemed to have been a meticulous Dutch recordkeeper with perfect handwriting.

Jack's lawyer-neighbor shared that I had a stepsister named Kathy who lived in Rochester. She was Gloria's daughter. Kathy was quite helpful when we had questions. She explained that her mom and Jack had married when she was a teenager. She was quite lovely and intelligent. But it was clear from the start that she hadn't liked my father. "Unpleasant," "unhappy," "alcoholic," and "verbally abusive" were some of the descriptions she used.

The trip also provided some clarity around what had happened with my mom. Apparently, Jack didn't leave of his own accord; he was asked to leave by my grandfather, who had seen enough of his son-in-law's drinking and abusive behavior toward his daughter and her two infants. Though there were many illuminating and sad moments like this, I was learning a lot about my biological father.

Amid the depressing revelations, there were also plenty of humorous moments, like when Ron and I went into the garage. Because of his many years at General Motors, Jack enjoyed a generous employee discount, which meant he had always owned great cars. Ron and I weren't surprised to find a new, perfectly kept white Buick Enclave parked there. As we looked around to see what else could be salvaged, we noticed a couple of glass sliding doors on the wall in front of the car. As soon as we opened them, a blast of cold air rushed into the hot, humid garage.

"Woah! Elvis in the house!" Ron said. We both started laughing.

The room was filled with Jack's extensive collection.

I have a stepsister, and my father loved Elvis?! What other shockers are in store?

Ron and I looked through the mostly junky paraphernalia honoring "The King," but thought maybe a few items could have some value. Kathy had told us that she wanted nothing from her parents' house, but Jack's lawyer-neighbor shadowed us constantly—I guess to make sure we didn't take anything. I found this humorous, given my history, or lack of history, with my father. I was only there because I had to be.

"The Elvis collection has been willed to your mom," Jack's lawyer-friend told us matter-of-factly.

"What the hell is my mom going to do with all this Elvis stuff from a man she despised?" I asked Ron later. We decided to ship it to my twin brother, Scott, who had once been a Rochester DJ, sound engineer, and musician. It seemed the best idea amid only awkward choices.

The secret garage room was also packed with many other items from Jack's life. He kept everything. We found pictures of me and my brother when we were little. The photos stopped at age ten or eleven. His visitation rights only lasted until we were three or four, and his involvement slowly trickled from little to nothing after that. There were also dozens of press clippings about me and my career on Wall Street.

"He always talked about you," Kathy told me, "especially when he got mad or frustrated with us. He'd say, 'My daughter would know how to do this.'"

My first thought was, *What a jerk!* But I was also astonished. He didn't seem the least bit interested in my career when we'd met all those years ago. Yet here were all these news clippings. *This father who barely spoke to me was proud of me?* It was all so confusing and honestly, a bit pitiful.

Ron and I also found a box filled with Jack's Korean War mementos. He was in the marines in that particularly short, brutal war. For the first time, I wondered if the drinking and messed-up behavior could be related. The photos clearly showed a soldier who had seen active combat. The picture of my father's sharp decline became clearer when we found photos and clippings from his childhood, which revealed a bright, active, popular, and happy young man. He'd played several sports, had good grades, and had been president of his high school class. Clearly, this was the man with whom my mom had fallen in love. It was certainly not the same bitter man I'd met for lunch. I stood there, wondering how such an accomplished young person could become an alcoholic and end up robbing a liquor store (true story). Jack's history was more complicated than I'd been told by my family as a child.

On a per capita basis, the Korean War was one of the bloodiest in modern times, leaving even seasoned soldiers devastated by the civilian and military casualties they'd witnessed. *Maybe he had post-traumatic stress disorder and never received the professional help he needed,* I speculated. The psychological support and resources that exist today weren't available when Jack came home from Korea in the 1950s. I began to see his life in a different light. But it was hard to be empathetic when Kathy shared stories about the harsh realities of her life with Jack. She seemed to have a good relationship with her mom but left home in her teens. Though she never said it directly, it seemed like Jack's behavior was a strong contributing factor in Kathy's early departure. I was happy we'd had a laugh about the Elvis stuff because everything else was just confusing and sad.

―――――

When we got back to Rochester, I had a long conversation with my mom about everything. We discussed giving the inheritance money to my brother Scott, but both wondered if he would accept anything from his estranged father.

"I don't know how to process any of this," Scott told us when we shared the news.

"I understand, Scott. Neither do we," I replied. "Just be happy you have that fight-to-survive Van Dusen DNA that kept us alive as preemies, but that Mom and our grandparents raised us instead of Jack. It was a true blessing that he wasn't in our lives."

Kathy is ten years older than I am, but we kept in touch for a while. She is kind and gracious. I felt for her. She went through a lot, and I admired her for never giving in to the anger and sadness she must have felt. I learned later that she had worked for a good friend of mine in a marketing role before retiring. Rochester might be a decent-size city, but it is still a small world.

The whole experience of meeting Kathy and going through my father's house had reinforced two ideas: First, I was so grateful for the amazing people who had raised me. Second, it's the people in our lives who make all the difference. My grandfather's life demonstrated the power of mentorship. Though not my birth father, he showed me everything necessary to live a full, happy, meaningful life and taught me about a world that was bigger than my own neighborhood and perspective. Supporting me through life's ups and downs, he was a model of hard work and expected it from me, too. My grandfather boosted my confidence, molded my beliefs and character, and gave me the strong foundation I needed. To this day, I still ask myself, *Where would I be without my family?* I certainly don't think it would be where I am today. I also remember regularly that I wasn't the only one who benefited from my grandfather's support and mentorship—people showed up in droves to pay their respects at his funeral. He was a wonderful human being. Every day I strive to contribute to the world the way he did.

My biological father might have left, but my life was enriched because caring people stepped in and filled the void with love and guidance. Many children aren't so lucky. They have no one to show them that there's another way, a *better* way, to live than the terrible things they witness and experience every day. It's one reason I am so passionate about mentorship. I never forget that my life could have been *very* different—that I was one of the lucky ones. It's why I sit on boards at a number of community colleges and scholarships funds, mentor girls through the YWCA, and support young professional women in finance, among other volunteer activities. I help organizations that give youths access to education, mentorship, health, and wellness—all are fundamental. My grandfather offered me these essentials and so much more, all without fanfare, every day of his life.

CHAPTER 13

A Scar Is a Souvenir
You Never Lose

"I don't want to die without any scars."

—Chuck Palahniuk

FOR MANY YEARS, MY HUSBAND RON AND I TRAVeled with two other couples. We never sat on a beach or by the pool. Instead, the six of us would get together and ask ourselves, "What is our next adventure?" We would often do things out West, usually involving a lot of mountain climbing and wine drinking.

One particular year, I remember our group took a trip to the Sierra Nevada Mountains in California. This stunning four-hundred-mile stretch of peaks is nicknamed the "Range of Light," thanks to the gorgeous and unusually light granite exposed on many of its summits. The giant sequoia trees that grow up to three hundred feet tall and Lake Tahoe, with its clear, thousand-foot-deep waters, are found here. It's also home to Yosemite National Park, long recognized as one of the most beautiful places in our country. I remember several moments during that trip when the views from some of the mountaintops rendered us all completely speechless. We were thousands of feet up, and the vistas were simply otherworldly.

Some of our hiking and climbing excursions took us above the elevation where bears roamed. That said, we did see fresh tracks from some species of large feline predator, possibly a mountain lion. We set up a base camp and from there, ascended the mountain on horseback. With our guide and cook, there were eight of us on horses and a whole mule train behind us with handlers and gear.

For some reason, every time I went on one of these trips, I ended up with the biggest horse, even though I was the smallest person in the group. It was scary for me to trust the horse as we wound our way up the mountains. You're on this narrow trail, and it takes the better part of a day to traverse it. Our group started out early in the morning, and the horses walked along the very edge of the treacherous switchbacks. Your gut instinct is to pull them back toward the canyon wall because you're looking down at a sheer drop of more than a thousand feet. But the animals are smart. They're well trained and, of course, they don't want to die, either.

"They like to walk along the edge," our guide told us, "because that is where the path is best for them."

When we got to a resting place, I half jokingly asked one of the handlers, "When was last time you lost anything over the edge?"

"Well," he said as he swallowed some water from his canteen, "we lost an entire mule train last week."

"Wow," I whispered. He was dead serious. *Okay,* I thought to myself, *I'm not going to ask him the logical follow-up question. Ignorance is bliss.*

At one point, I took my hands, put them on the back of my saddle, closed my eyes, and said out loud, "God, please watch over me. I don't want to die this way."

I repeated a mantra all the way up the mountain: *Trust the horse. Trust the horse. Trust the horse.*

Ron, an avid hunter who had taken many trips to middle-of-nowhere mountain ranges, was a seasoned outdoorsman. He was absolutely in his element on this trip. Despite my moments of fear, the whole experience was spectacular. It was one of the greatest trips we ever took together. The trail guides and handlers brought us from our base camp all the way up to ten thousand feet, dropped us off in the remote wilderness, and took our horses back down. The plan was for them to come back for us a full week later.

We settled in and decided to climb and rappel a rock face. Our friend Scott would take the lead on this activity because he was an expert rock climber and was a friend of the famous Royal Robbins, one of the pioneers of American rock climbing. We started out on belay, using hooks and ropes. We'd use our fingers and toes to find little crevices to slowly climb the rock face. The goal was to get to the top, then rappel back down. I'd only done this a couple of times but knew that rappelling down was supposed to be the easy part. But I didn't realize the granite was razor sharp. As I rappelled down, I went sideways, which threw me off-kilter. I slammed into the granite cliff and sliced open my hand. It would not stop bleeding. Clearly, I needed stiches, but we were too far away from civilization and any type of medical center or hospital. We cleaned my wound and wrapped it as best we could.

"Well, you're definitely going to have a scar," Scott said, "but you can tell people you didn't get it in a rose garden!"

I laughed, even though the gash smarted. "I guess I'll never be a hand model, but who cares. I'll look at my scar and always remember this adventure."

The place was too beautiful to let my mishap interfere. Every day was full of refreshing activities and awe-inspiring nature. It was exhilarating and peaceful. At night, I slept deeply and peacefully underneath a star-filled sky. My Ranger Ron hubby had provided the two of us with all the right equipment, so we were as comfortable as we could be, considering we were sleeping on granite.

One morning after a late night, we decided to hike up a small summit nearby. When we got up to the top, we sat down and ate peanut butter and jelly sandwiches, quietly enjoying the amazing vistas all around us. I was ravenous, and in that moment those PB&J sandwiches were like the best thing I'd ever tasted in my life. And that view! It was so spectacular. In the distance, we heard cow bells and looked way, way down into the valley. We couldn't believe it. We could actually see a rancher with his cattle nearly ten thousand feet below us. That's how clear the cold, crisp air overlooking Yosemite is. Every day at 5:00 p.m., we'd navigate our way to this large plateau-like rock formation in the middle of a small glacial lake. We called it Cocktail Rock. We'd swim out, open tin cans of sardines or smoked oysters, sit around a campfire, and drink wine or beer. It was heaven on earth.

I've never been one to sit on the sidelines of life, particularly when it comes to exploring nature, the outdoors, trying new sports and activities, or testing my physical and mental limits. This keeps life interesting. Ron and I were lucky to share a love of the outdoors and an active lifestyle. And whenever I'm having a bad day, I look at the little scar on my hand that's the perfect souvenir of a very special memory together.

CHAPTER 14

Don't Build Your Own Prison

"Grief is like a long valley, a winding valley where any bend may reveal a totally new landscape."

—C. S. Lewis

RON AND I HAD THIRTY YEARS TOGETHER BEFORE he took his own life.

Our marriage wasn't perfect, but our life together was full of love and joy. I was the lucky one. My troubled father left early, and my grandparents stepped in to help my mom raise me and my brother in a supportive, happy home. Unfortunately, Ron's dad stuck around, dispensing a daily dose of violence and abuse to him and his mother for decades.

It's certainly possible to overcome childhood trauma—many people have—but not alone. Though it's a great teacher, adversity is a formidable opponent. No one can climb all of life's mountains alone.

We forget that grace is always there, freely offered. We just have to love ourselves enough to surrender to its constant, unconditional acceptance and guidance. It's an infinite source of spiritual renewal and continuous rebirth.

Ron tried so hard to accept grace but never felt worthy. He was blameless but blamed himself. This is the wretched curse of the abused. He was great at supporting others but had trouble asking for or receiving help himself. He climbed a lot of mountains and battled a lot of demons alone. It didn't have to be that way. He was surrounded by people who loved him. Grace was all around, inside and out, if only he'd been open to it.

Ron never wanted to talk about his father or his feelings.

"Lor, my father took up too much of my life," he'd say. "I don't want to waste another minute on him."

I respected this wish because I didn't have anything good to say about my own biological father. But I did have many happy stories to share about my childhood; my husband had none. He tried so hard to bridge that gap, pouring himself into fatherhood and making sure that his sons had the wonderful childhood he'd never known. He was an adoring husband, regularly writing me love notes and making sure I felt treasured in ways his mother had never experienced. He had spent much of his life protecting his mother from his father's fists. As an adult, he would wear himself out, protecting family and friends with his entire being. He just forgot to protect himself.

Ron loved all of us with his big, wounded heart, but could never fully let us in. Expert at masking his feelings, he always looked perfect on the outside. Handsome, healthy, and intimidatingly fit— that's what he let the world see. At home, his profound sadness manifested in different ways. Debilitating depression, mood swings, and anger would bubble up out of the blue and ruin his day until he managed to suppress the sadness one more time.

When I look back now, I see things more clearly. For example, there was constantly turbulence around the holidays. My big Italian family always had people over to celebrate, so for me it was a joyful time of year. We would have a big open house on Christmas Eve and invite a hundred people or so. But there was always a fight beforehand. It was as if Ron was looking for an opportunity to start something. He'd say, "We're not doing this again this year, right?" Back then, I couldn't grasp why he hated such wonderful holiday gatherings. Our house was filled with laughter and holiday cheer. Now, I understand that his holiday memories must have been horrifying. What brought me joy was a trigger for him. What filled my cup, drained his.

The ups and downs weren't easy, and I remember saying to my mom a couple of times, "I can't do this anymore." She'd advise me to work things out, to stay together despite our struggles. My family loved Ron, and he loved them.

Family was always first, and so Ron and I muddled through our challenges as a couple. But I don't think any of us fully understood the epic battles Ron was fighting alone inside his heart and head every day of his life. We knew he struggled but never thought he'd give up. His close friends were shocked when they heard that Ron had taken his own life. None of us ever saw any indications that this was something he would even consider.

I now understand that this is often the case. My husband's biggest mistake was believing that because he'd survived childhood trauma, he could live with it. Those toxic masculine voices in his head, which had been handed down to him by his father, told Ron to shove down the pain; it was all in the past. Unfortunately, that's not how trauma works. Coping is not a sustainable plan—and it's definitely not a treatment. Ironically, he finally sought professional help in the last few months of his life, after decades of me asking him to reach out. I often wonder if things would have turned out differently if he'd sought help earlier.

After Ron died, I knew that *I* needed the professional help I hadn't sought when I was raped as a graduate student at Harvard. Back then, times were different. I was also too young, afraid, and ashamed to seek help. That was a mistake. Miraculously, I made it through. But I could have lost everything I'd worked for. Today, as a more mature adult, I'm not willing to gamble with my mental health anymore. I've seen too many people lose this bet. Through counseling, I came to realize that there's no moving on from trauma and grief; you have to learn how to integrate the pain into your life so that you can start to function again and put one foot in front of the other. I didn't understand this before therapy. Everyone's time-line for healing is different, but I learned that resilience is possible. I learned that you can stop fighting against the devastating pain so it doesn't turn into lifelong suffering. This requires what therapists call "radical acceptance." The blog for Skyland Trail, published by a mental health treatment organization based in Atlanta, describes the term well:

> Radical acceptance is when you stop fighting reality, stop responding with impulsive or destructive be-haviors when things aren't going the way you want them to, and let go of bitterness that may be keeping you trapped in a cycle of suffering.

Another wellness site, Hopeway.org, says, "Radical acceptance is a distress tolerance skill that is designed to keep pain from turning into suffering."

Very few lives go untouched by grief or other traumatic forms of adversity. They are part of the human experience. But don't let fear, shame, arrogance, bitterness, or any other negative emotion keep you from living the life you were meant to live. Radical acceptance worked for me, but there are many approaches to therapy. What's important is to seek professional help when needed, do the hard work, give yourself the necessary time to heal, and be open to the grace that is all around you.

COVID-19 had a devastating effect on Ron. He was very anxious about contracting the disease, so he kept himself isolated for a long time. I, on the other hand, was trying to manage a business through unprecedented times, which meant more travel. I didn't realize it at the time, but it was a lethal combination.

On the day Ron took his life, Father's Day 2020, I was in Florida with a return flight home the next morning. Ron had plans to spend the afternoon with our oldest son, Conner. When Ron didn't show up, we all knew that something was wrong. It took nearly twelve hours for the police to find Ron's body at his favorite local hunting spot out in the woods. None of us could process the news. Conner kept asking, "Wasn't time with me enough to keep him alive?" It was heartbreaking.

The feelings of guilt were overwhelming. *Could I have stopped this if I'd been home? For God's sake, how can I read a room full of investors, board members, and analysts, but not my husband's heart?* We'd had a stupid little argument about changing our health care plan on the phone the morning of his death. I didn't understand why he was so upset. It seemed so trivial to me, but he was really mad. I don't like confrontation. Unlike Ron, I hadn't grown up with a man yelling at me. My grandfather was a calm, plainspoken person. Ron's family dynamic was toxic and volatile, which made our dynamic as a couple complex.

"Ron, the health care plan has already been changed. I'm sorry, but it's done."

After the conversation, he texted me one word: "Goodbye." This was his suicide note. *Did I push Ron over the edge?* In the wake of a loved one's suicide, these are the irrational thoughts and questions that haunt you.

None of us will ever fully understand what happened that day. Ron was always impulsive, and I choose to believe his suicide was an impulsive, irrational act. He was having a bad day and had access to a lot of guns. He must have left in a hurry because there were steaks left out on the counter for his meal with Conner later that day. I can't imagine that Ron would have followed through if he had stopped for even a second to consider the excruciating pain his death would cause the people he loved. Thankfully, I believe in an afterlife where souls who struggle on this earth can finally find peace. Ron was one of those souls, and I wouldn't be able to cope if I believed otherwise.

I was devastated by the loss of my husband. I couldn't eat, sleep, or function. Luckily, my boys and I could grieve together because the COVID-19 pandemic allowed them to work remotely from our family home for a couple of months. This was a true gift. I really don't know how I would have survived without their support. They were my rocks and handled everything. Three of my closest girlfriends also pitched in, managing the details around the funeral and wake. My boys and my friends circled around me, protected me from questions, and held me up through the horror of it all.

To this day, I'm not comfortable talking about Ron's suicide with strangers. People ask, "Are you divorced?" They assume I'm too young to be a widow.

One acquaintance even asked, "Did you know your husband was going to do this?"

Really?

I've become a master at protecting myself. For interviews and in preparation for public events, I rehearse my answers. This way, I'm not triggered by a surprising question. Practice allows me to reply honestly and with dignity, so I can honor my husband's memory without opening up a wound so deep it still stops my heart some days.

Before Ron left us, he did a lot of good in this world. Not only did he love me, his boys, and our extended family, but he was also the go-to guy in his friend group—reliable, earnest, and caring. Active in the community and the lives of his boys, I swear he coached every school sports team in town—even after his sons were grown. He always went the extra mile—mentoring players, showing up for anyone who needed a ride to a game or a friendly face in the stands. If someone couldn't afford the necessary sports equipment, Ron bought it for them. As a longtime board member at a community child advocacy center supporting abused and neglected children, he tried to make the world a better place for those most in need. Ron brightened many lives with his contagious laugh and kind, generous spirit. There are so many people mourning the loss of this special human being.

———

They say that time is a great healer. Slowly, joy is coming back into my life. Every day is still hard, but I try to focus on a brighter future. Profound life events change you in ways you never expect. I'm not as light as I used to be, but am deeper, more thoughtful, and more empathetic. I treasure every human experience and am more grateful than ever for my life and family. My suffering does not make me unique or special. Like so many others who have experienced tragedy, life offers a simple choice: to harden our hearts to a cruel world or open our hearts to the suffering of others. I choose the latter and believe I've already been able to help others who have lost loved ones, especially to suicide.

Let me be honest, though, there have been plenty of rough days. Fourth of July weekend 2021, a year after Ron's death, was particularly difficult. Independence Day had always been a huge holiday for our family. Full of traditions, this day was always filled with a long weekend stay at our lake house, fireworks and cookouts, and our annual trip to Tanglewood in Lenox, Massachusetts for an outdoor concert. Though many caring friends invited me to spend the holiday weekend with them after Ron's death, I didn't have the energy to accept. I was grateful for the invitations but felt that being part of a big, happy family gathering might make me feel worse. I was still depressed. For so many years, it had been my family celebrating together. This year, our family traditions were not meant to be. Conner was visiting friends. Cole had to stay in Los Angeles for work. Even Grace, our precious black Lab who had been my constant companion after Ron's death, was no longer with me. She had died suddenly only eleven months after Ron. With unconditional love, she had seen me through my darkest hours of grief, and now she wasn't at my side. Losing her was brutal—and having to tell my boys the news over the phone had been excruciating. After we'd all sobbed uncontrollably, we reflected on all the great memories of her seven years with us, especially when we brought her home as a puppy.

"Conner, remember when you suggested we call her Grace? I asked, 'Why Grace?' and you said, 'Grace is something you get that you don't deserve.'"

I'll never forget that. She really was our unexpected gift.

Drowning in all the memories and fighting back the loneliness that July Fourth, I decided not to mope around the lake house. I would distract myself the healthy way and go into town for a yoga class. I dressed, got in my car, and started driving up the dirt road. Fighting back tears, I moaned, "I don't even have a dog!" The moment the words left my lips, I started laughing. *Lori, that is so pathetic! Time to leave your pity party.* As soon as I arrived at yoga class, my mood shifted. Before class even started, my phone rang. Some longtime clients who had become friends were FaceTiming from Italy. They knew how important the holiday was to me and called to sing me a song to cheer me up. Nicky, their godson, had just had his first baby and proudly introduced me. It was a very joyful conversation and lifted my spirits.

The yoga class was amazing and rejuvenating. Pity was replaced by renewed energy and hope. Afterward, another friend called from Australia, then later, more friends and family. Everyone made me laugh and smile. I didn't feel alone anymore. I was grateful for all the support and realized I had to start putting one foot in front of the other again, literally. Daily exercise—yoga, walking, and running—had always been a priority, but now these activities would become sacrosanct, as would the act of expressing my gratitude out loud every day.

These habits made all the difference. Now, when I finish running, I often feel compelled to write notes about the ideas that come to me while I'm soaking up the natural, positive energy of the world around me. I breathe and take a few moments to appreciate the strength of my own beating heart. There's something about exercise—about attending to my physical well-being—that puts me on the right frequency. The ideas that come to me are not my own; they're just small signatures revealing how I'm being worked on by a force much greater than myself. In these moments, I know that Ron is now part of that perfect, all-loving life force and will always be with me in spirit.

In addition to yoga and running, reading meditations became an important daily ritual. Sipping hot tea and reading has become a centering and thought-provoking start to my day. Trust me, it's so much better than opening emails first thing; talk about an instant stress trigger!

In one of my readings last year, I came upon a simple, powerful legend from the Middle Ages. It was about a prisoner who had been behind bars in a dark, dreary dungeon for twenty years. His only interaction with the outside world was when his jailer pushed open the thick, heavy, iron-and-wood cell door once a day to bring him bread and water. After so many years alone in the dark, the prisoner decided he couldn't take it anymore. The next time his jailer came, he planned to jump him and be killed so he could end his misery. In preparation for the encounter, the prisoner pushed on the handle of the massive door and found it unlocked. Bewildered, he cautiously walked out into the hall, where he passed several guards who made no attempt to stop him. Next, he walked out into the bright morning sunlight. His eyes could barely handle the sunlight after so many years of darkness. After a moment of adjustment, he carefully walked across the great prison yard, breathing in the various smells of the grass and flowers for the first time in so long. Again, the guards barely noticed him. Finally, the prisoner walked right out the front gates and reentered a world he hadn't seen in decades. For twenty years, the man had been a captive—not of the prison—but of his own false belief that he was a captive.

Life is hard, and we must give ourselves the grace to heal, but so many of us build our own prisons. We become captives to life's inevitable pain, sorrow, and frustration. We want to give up, stop pushing forward, stop trying, stop growing. It doesn't have to be this way. Don't build your own prison. "Our life is what our thoughts make it," Marcus Aurelius wrote in *Meditations*. I know this to be true. When life is difficult—even unbearably so—don't choose to stay in the darkness. Push open the door, let in other people and the light, and put one foot in front of the other. And while you're helping yourself, take what you've learned in the darkness and help another human being back to the light. This is what gives our lives meaning.

CHAPTER 15

Shape Your Life One Step at a Time

"The most difficult thing is the decision
to act. The rest is merely tenacity."

—*Amelia Earhart*

IT'S AN EARLY SUMMER MORNING ON THE FINGER
Lakes. Thump. Thump. Thump. One . . . foot . . . in . . . front . . .
of . . . the . . . other . . . Alone in nature, I breathe in the moist, still-
cool air and listen to the mournful cry of a loon across the inlet. For
me, running is meditation in motion. Immersed in all the beauty of
the present moment, I am at peace and so very grateful to be here
for a long weekend with my sons. These glacial lakes have held a
special place in our hearts for twenty-five years. When we are here,
life really doesn't get any better.

As night departs and the first rays of sunlight shimmer on the water, I do not know what the future will bring, and that's okay. It's not something I can control, so I've learned to let it go. For now, the steady rhythm of my feet moving across the earth and each measured breath mingling with the morning mist are enough. A deep, quiet joy washes over me.

Eleanor Roosevelt once famously said, "In the long run, we shape our lives, and we shape ourselves. The process never ends until we die. And the choices we make are ultimately our own responsibility."

We *are* our choices. Each day presents new opportunities and challenges—large and small. Our responses to both create our reality. None of us can rid our lives of adversity. It's an ever-present companion. All we can do is be intentional in our thoughts and behaviors, find wisdom in each challenge, and stay true to our beliefs. Avoid worry and regret, and give yourself the time and grace you need to process failure or loss. You can't skip this necessary step. But try with all your heart to remain hopeful and resilient, even when the situation seems impossible. It is this mindset that makes all the difference.

Despite life's inevitable challenges, we must find the courage each day to embrace opportunities that allow us to share our unique gifts with the world. Do not withhold your unique gifts when it is within your power to act and have a positive impact. Be brave, for it is in the giving of ourselves that we receive. Accept the divine grace within you and all around you. Let it be a source of eternal light and hope.

When life becomes difficult, the knee-jerk reaction is often anger, fear, or self-pity, especially when we are tired, hungry, stressed out, or overworked. When we feel depleted, it's just easier to blame others or our circumstances. "I could have reached that goal, if only this hadn't happened," we tell ourselves. If you follow this path, you will waste time and energy, and struggle to grow. You can't take a single experience or human relationship out of your history. They all play a role in your unique life journey. You can't have a better past, only a richer present, which in turn creates a better future. Everything and everyone that you have experienced has been there for a reason. If you want to find your calling, pay close attention to this continuum.

We have all had life punch us square in the face. Many of us have been punched over and over again. It doesn't seem fair. To deal with suffering, we have to feel the pain and admit how much we are hurting. But we can't let it harden our hearts. We can't let the anguish or fear destroy who we are. The universe isn't trying to punish us. There's an opportunity for growth somewhere in all that pain. The great humanitarian Mother Teresa once said, "Life is a song, sing it. Life is a struggle, accept it." Serving those dealing with poverty, HIV/AIDS, leprosy, and tuberculosis, Mother Teresa's work was extremely difficult, but it was filled with meaning and purpose. She persevered and changed the world for many disenfranchised people.

We must allow ourselves to be broken down sometimes in order to discover our purest humanity. For thousands of years, miners have used fire to refine gold. The heat liquifies the gold, allowing for the separation and removal of everything that is not gold. The result is 99.5 percent pure gold. Adversity is like the heat, refining our essence, removing everything that is not our truest, most beautiful and authentic selves. What type of life do we create if we choose anger, pity, or negativity? This state of mind is rarely productive or healthy. It's okay to be sad or mad, to grieve and cry; it's a necessary part of healing. Be kind to yourself and take the time you need. After Ron's death, I read a powerful book about grieving called *It's OK That You're Not OK: Meeting Grief and Loss in a Culture That Doesn't Understand* by Megan Devine. The title says it all. As a therapist and a widow, the author recommends that you give yourself permission to feel what you feel and do what you need to do to find a healthy path. Have faith that life will get better, and as soon as you feel able, start putting one foot in front of the other again.

How do we strengthen ourselves to face life's inevitable challenges? I believe self-acceptance, strong relationships, self-care, and a noble purpose provide a strong foundation. We must love ourselves enough to prioritize our spiritual, emotional, and physical well-being every day—no matter how busy we are. Remember to be for yourself the person you are for others. You matter. Taking care of yourself with healthy relationships and habits is important. I could not get through my day without a run, walk, or yoga, as well as time for meditation, family, and friends. This simple wisdom took me *years* to learn. Everybody needs space to think, slow down, laugh, talk with others, and just breathe. We must choose to make space in our lives.

Honestly, think about the alternative: continuously spinning from one thing to the next without ever stopping. It's like being on a hamster wheel. That's an unhealthy choice that creates an unhealthy life. Unfortunately, it's a reality for all too many people in today's busy world. Turn off the phone. Step away from the computer. Leave work at the office. Meet a friend for coffee. Have dinner with your family. Get outside, move, and breathe the fresh air. Go for a walk and enjoy nature. Observe. Find what grounds you. Be thankful for what you have. Don't focus on what you've lost. Find your center. Living and working ethically, purposefully, and meaningfully requires balance. It's not always easy to achieve, but it's crucial to keep trying.

While I was writing this book, one of my closest friends sent me a passage from *A Gentle Reminder*, written by author and poet Bianca Sparacino. It touched me deeply, so I'd like to share it with you:

> I think it's beautiful—the way you show up in this world, unguarded and willing to try again, despite all the ways it has tried to defeat you. I think it's beautiful. The way you tuck courage into yourself each morning, the way you refuse to be anything but hopeful in this world, despite the inner battles you fight, despite the struggles you have experienced for so long. I think it's beautiful—the way you twist your losses into lessons, the way you fight even when

you feel weak. You are not weak. There is a resounding level of courage to be found in being the person who continues to heal, even when it hurts. There is a resounding level of bravery to be found in being the person who believes in the light, even when they cannot see it.

Darkness does not exist by itself. It is nothing more than the absence of light. Night will come, and so will a new day. This is the only promise life makes. So it has been, and so it shall always be. Trust the journey's ups and downs and embrace the divine wisdom in both.

AFTERWORD

AS I WAS FINISHING THE FINAL DRAFT OF THE MAN-
uscript for this book, my mother, Alice, was hospitalized and diagnosed with terminal lung cancer. She had clearly been battling the
disease for a while without any of us realizing it, even her. She died
within twenty-four hours of entering the hospital. It was a complete
shock to all of us.

I am grateful that until the very end, she lived a happy, full
life, getting together with her family and friends, and at home with
her many beloved dogs. After her death, I was collecting some of
her things and found a printed dish towel hanging in her kitchen.
It read, "The list of people I want to meet. Number 1: Dogs." It
made me smile and think about my own dog, Grace, whom all of
us had adored.

Alice Van Dusen was a modest, witty, kind soul—and completely devoted to her family. I believe she battled through her de-
clining health quietly and stoically in order to support my boys and
me through the loss of Ron in 2020. It was just like her to put others
first, especially me. Do you remember all those times as a child when
your mother tucked you in, kissed away your pain, and reminded
you that everything would be all right? My mother did this for me
until her final day on earth. In fact, she was texting me about a work
trip only two days before she was hospitalized. Even the night before
she passed, she was giving me advice on work and travel plans from

her hospital bed. She never wavered in her love, care, and protection, even when she was suffering. Spiritually, she has held my hand every day of my life, and I am so grateful that we were together, holding hands, when she passed.

As the divorced, working mother of twins in the 1960s, my mother faced a type of isolation and discrimination that is much less common for American women today. She was part of a humble, independent, and determined generation that forged significant change, not always as activists, but more often quietly as strong women working hard to create more opportunities for their children and grandchildren. This was my mom to a T. As I was growing my financial advisory business as a woman in a man's world, my mom was always my right hand. Personally, professionally, or spiritually, I wouldn't be where I am today without her. She was my rock.

I believe we exist to create a better world through the lives we live—a world filled with peace, justice, kindness, love, and compassion. This is the definition of grace, and it was how my mom lived every day of her life. Wherever I traveled throughout the world, people knew my mom and would ask about her. "We love Alice. How is she?" Through simple, daily acts of kindness and connection, she left the world a better place than she found it. I hope to do the same in honor of my amazing role model.

Rest in peace, Mom. I will miss you every minute of every day until we see each other again.

ACKNOWLEDGMENTS

WRITING A BOOK IS NO SMALL TASK, AND I HAVE A number of people to thank for their help on this journey.

To my sons Conner and Cole Boillat, thank you both for your constant love and care. Cole, thanks for your helpful observations and edits. You definitely enriched the story while providing support and humor along the way.

To my late husband Ron for his encouragement, kindness, and adoration throughout our thirty-year marriage. I know you are not here to read these words, but I hope you know how many people still miss you terribly every day, including me.

To my late mother Alice Van Dusen, who passed away just as I was finishing *Running with Grace*. Mom, thank you for a lifetime of unwavering love and support. You taught me to tap into the grace that is all around, even in the toughest of times. I still feel your presence daily.

To my dear girlfriends, Kelly, Malisa, Theresa M., Theresa N., and Susan for their care and protection as I found the courage to share my story. Your friendship and support have meant the world to me.

To my close friend Dr. Ian Wilson, for being a sounding board and providing creative guidance.

To my beta readers, especially Doug VanOort, thank you for the advice, time, and counsel—all were a big help.

To our team at LVW Advisors, I'd like to express my immense gratitude for your constant support, dedication, and professionalism.

A special shout out to my former colleague John Martin for helping me revisit some of the financial details of the Bernie Madoff story.

And, finally, thank you to Kathy Meis and the team at Bublish for helping me bring my story to life.

ABOUT THE AUTHOR

LORI VAN DUSEN, CIMA, IS THE FOUNDER AND CEO of LVW Advisors, an award-winning registered investment advisory firm that serves both wealthy families and individuals, as well as nonprofit institutions throughout the United States. An advocate of client-focused strategies for more than twenty-five years, she has become the voice of reason for providing unbiased, integrated solutions in a fragmented financial services industry. Lori is passionate about numerous philanthropic causes, serving on several boards focused on urban education, health and wellness, and the fine arts.

Lori began her investment advisory career in 1987 with Shearson Lehman Brothers, which was later acquired by Citigroup Smith Barney. By 2004, she had achieved the title of managing director with Citigroup Smith Barney. In a pioneering move, she assumed the role of co-lead at a large RIA, overseeing $8 billion dollars in assets under management. She founded LVW Advisors in 2011.

A recipient of numerous accolades, Lori was most recently named to *Barron's* Hall of Fame, which recognizes financial advisors who have appeared in ten or more of *Barron's* annual Top 100 Advisor rankings. Additionally, Lori was ranked for the third year in a row No. 3 in *Forbes'* 2021 Best-In-State Wealth Advisors list. Lori has also been ranked No. 66 in *Forbes'* 2021, 2020, and 2019 America's Top Wealth Advisors, and in the top five by *Forbes* in both the 2021 and 2020 America's Top Women Wealth Advisors lists.

In recognition of her involvement in the Rochester community, Lori was inducted into the 2019 Rochester Business Hall of Fame and joins a prestigious list of Rochester business leaders who have been previously inducted. Lori has also been recognized by the Girl Scouts of Western New York as one of the 2019 Women of Distinction.

Lori has served on many boards and committees in the past. She currently serves on the following boards: F.F. Thompson Health, Memorial Art Gallery Board of Managers, Monroe Community College Foundation, Rochester Area Community Foundation, and the University of Rochester Medical Center. Lori also sits on the advisory board for Institutional Investor's RIA Institute.

Lori was one of the leaders of the Association of Professional Investment Consultants and one of the founders of Citigroup Institutional Consulting. She holds the Certified Investment Management Analyst designation, administered by the Investments & Wealth Institute® in conjunction with The Wharton School. Lori received her undergraduate degree from Ithaca College and a Master of Education from Harvard University.

A native of Rochester, New York, Lori is a long-distance runner and an avid yogi, and enjoys decorating and savoring the area's local music scene. She regularly cooks and hosts large Italian meals for her family and friends.

Milton Keynes UK
Ingram Content Group UK Ltd.
UKHW021036131123
432473UK00014B/308/J